BACKPACKER

TED ALVAREZ

THE SURVIVAL
HACKER'S
HANDBOOK

HOW TO SURVIVE WITH JUST ABOUT ANYTHING

BACKPACKER

THE SURVIVAL

HACKER'S

HANDBOOK

How to Survive with

Just About Anything

Ted Alvarez

GUILFORD, CONNECTICUT

FALCONGUIDES®

An imprint of The Rowman & Littlefield Publishing Group, Inc.
4501 Forbes Blvd., Ste. 200
Lanham, MD 20706
Falcon and FalconGuides are registered trademarks and Make Adventure Your Story is a trademark
of The Rowman & Littlefield Publishing Group, Inc.

Distributed by NATIONAL BOOK NETWORK
Copyright © 2018 *BACKPACKER* magazine, a division of Active Interest Media
All illustrations by Robert Prince

British Library Cataloguing in Publication Information available
Library of Congress Cataloging-in-Publication Data on file.

ISBN 978-1-4930-3056-9
ISBN 978-1-4930-3057-6 (e-book)

∞™ The paper used in this publication meets the minimum requirements of American National
Standard for Information Sciences—Permanence of Paper for Printed Library Materials, ANSI/NISO
Z39.48-1992.

Printed in the United States of America

CONTENTS

INTRODUCTION

Who Is a Survivor?

This is a question our species has been answering, with varying degrees of success, for hundreds of thousands of years. Trial and error has kept us out of the mouths of beasts and canyons long enough to invent the deep pleasures of binge TV and discover the deeper pleasures of recreational outdoor adventure.

But you could be forgiven for thinking a survivor doesn't look like you. Media representations bring us he-men with exotic accents who guzzle songbirds and take inexcusable-except-in-Hollywood risks. Shoeless Anglo shamans promise to share the True Ancient Wisdom, and (perhaps worst of all) there are the crying pretenders: naked, afraid, and dysenterically spewing from both ends after making the most basic mistakes.

Several years ago, I began writing a column for *BACKPACKER* magazine called "Survival Lab." It was "survival for the rest of us"—a reaction to the sensationalism of über-survivor culture, a quest to empower the regular gal or guy to ignore all the silliness and find what really works. My qualifications? I didn't have any—and that was the point. The thinking was if a doofus like me couldn't pull it off in controlled situations, then it could hardly be counted on in times of crisis. But in the process of combining the best of bushcrafting holy writ with improvised solutions, I had to try almost everything once. So I did. From sleeping in leaf beds and lean-tos to prove which offers a better night's sleep to sussing out precisely why drinking your pee in the desert is a terrible idea, I went whole guinea pig on myself.

I earned all kinds of useful insights and busted plenty of myths for the average outdoor adventurer in that process. For example, starting a friction fire with two sticks and zero practice leads to hair-rending frustration at best and hypothermia at worst. Better idea: Never enter the backcountry without two lighters and a pack of waterproof matches. But that climbing legend about using a frozen Snickers bar for a snow anchor? That one actually works—provided you've got only one person on the rope and you don't fall more than once.

That's not to say there isn't wisdom to be found in the old ways. Learning how to bring flame or conjure water from nothing like a magical caveman instills a deep confidence and comfort in the outdoors. And in a true survival situation, when calm and reserves of grit will save the day quicker than any piece of dedicated CYA survival gear, understanding precisely what you can handle and how you'd handle it is even more valuable.

Humans are constant experimentalists. We build on old knowledge with the new. Knowing how to use a candy wrapper to flag down a rescue helicopter can be just as important as being able to build a fire. The only reason our species is around is because we are inveterate tinkerers, restless MacGyvers who experiment with everything from medicinal plants to carbon fiber. The aggregate knowledge is survival, and the unification of ancient techniques, modern theory, and relentless practice creates the ultimate survivor. Survivors are the original hackers.

That's you, reading this handbook right now. There's an unbroken genetic line stretching from you back through time to your ancestors, who hacked survival successfully across land bridges and snowy wastes and even the eighties, when a mobile phone was the size of a loaf of bread. You are their legacy, and you have what it takes by virtue of being alive now—whether you're clinging to the side of K2 or hunkered down in a cozy coffee shop.

This also includes the contributors to BACKPACKER magazine, where world-class survivalists and outdoor writers with deep experience in the field—some of it harrowing—have pooled their knowledge for decades. I've collected the best they have to offer and added my own hard-won experience to create The Survival Hacker's Handbook.

I'm after more than just regurgitating the 10 Essentials—though they are a solid foundation for building survival best practices. (Here's a lightning-round refresher: food, water, compass and map, fire-starting kit, light source, waterproof and insulating layers, first aid kit, knife or multitool, sun protection, and an emergency shelter like a survival blanket.) But they're worthless if you just toss them in your pack and don't know how to use them—or if the unforgiving mind game of survival scrambles your priorities, and you forget the no-brainers like eating, drinking, or finding shelter.

To help you keep those priorities in order, I've organized this book around an ingenious bit of survival shorthand passed on to me by the toughest bastard I know. (This is someone who taught me how to survive for days on little more than mice and cactus. It's not as delicious as it sounds.) Call it the Rule of 15: In critical conditions, you can survive about 15 minutes without shelter, 15 hours without water, 15 days without food, and 15 months without being found. If you can continually satisfy the first three, you could, of course, survive longer than 15 months, but that's probably the point at which seasons repeat and you start talking to rocks—no way to live at all. Accordingly, the first half of this book is built in order of necessity (shelter, fire, water, food, lost); the second half concentrates on the interruptive forces that can compromise or overrule any of your bedrock tasks at any point if they are serious enough (injury, threats, mindset, fitness). Just absorbing and remembering this sequence is a form of empowerment that takes the guesswork out and orders your focus before you even step outside.

About that: Don't forget to get outdoors to practice. The tips and techniques contained herein all work, but they work *so much better* after you've tested them in the field, on your own terms, and determined which type of survival hacker you are, whether that's a tech-shortcut pragmatist or bushcrafty native skills revivalist. Successful survival is a highly individual expression of personality.

Just don't drink your own pee. Seriously.

> *Thirst trumps waterborne microorganisms in a survival situation. Drink up.* Credit: istockphoto

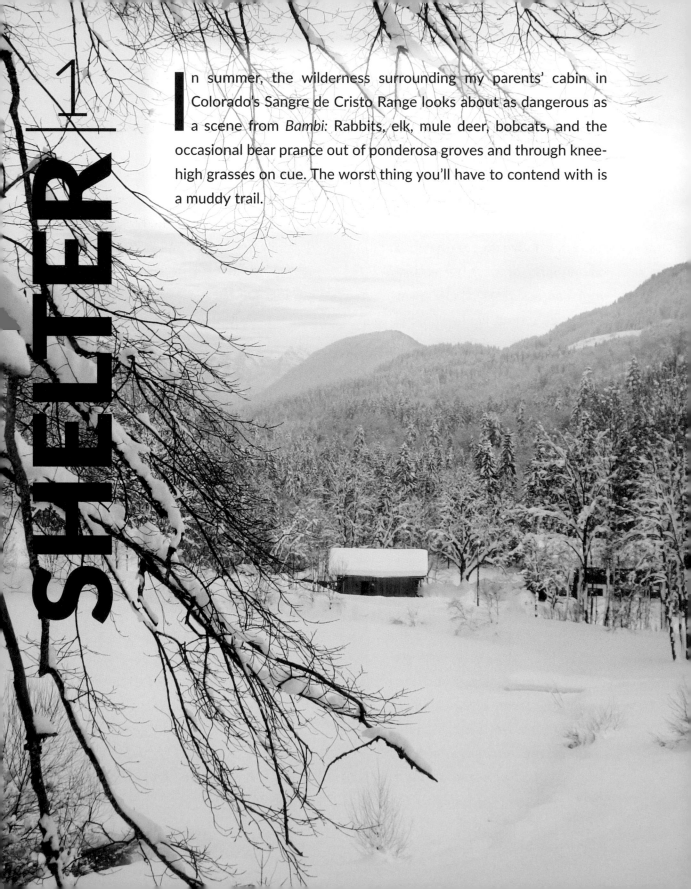

SHELTER

1

In summer, the wilderness surrounding my parents' cabin in Colorado's Sangre de Cristo Range looks about as dangerous as a scene from *Bambi*: Rabbits, elk, mule deer, bobcats, and the occasional bear prance out of ponderosa groves and through knee-high grasses on cue. The worst thing you'll have to contend with is a muddy trail.

But winter brings short days and cold nights. The few human inhabitants pack up for warmer climates, creeks freeze in the negative-degree temps, and 7-foot-high snowdrifts hunch over road corners like sleeping polar bears, sealing the place off.

To most people.

But my family is a different breed, unable to resist the total solitude, spindrift spiraling through tree-filtered sunlight, an endless carpet of powder—and the promise of a fire to chase out the chill. Crossing the 7 frozen miles from highway to cabin has become a New Year's tradition for my family ten years running. Over that time and those miles, we've learned the value of the Winter Siege, the all-hands approach that turns winter epics into fireside stories.

On one early winter attempt, our tank-tracked ATV bogged down on a particularly heinous snowdrift 2 miles in. We'd left at 10 a.m.—plenty of time, we thought—but no amount of technique or brute force could dislodge the doomed vehicle from its grave. So we ditched it, strapped on snowshoes, and prepared to haul as many supplies as we could stuff into our packs, prioritizing the beer and wine. Midafternoon sun gave us confidence we had enough light for the 5 miles of untrodden snow ahead.

Breaking trail through deep snow and up steep grades takes a toll, and it didn't take long for my late-50-something parents' pace to slacken. Then my mom caught a snowshoe and fell, twisting a knee already weakened by old ski injuries. As that happened, the sun slipped behind Blanca Peak for good, ushering in deep purples and cold winds. The change from afternoon hike to evening epic was fast: We had 2 miles to go, it was dark, and my mom could only hobble a few feet per minute before stopping to wince and rest.

We inched across crusted slabs while the wind raked us raw. Jeff, my twenty-three-year-old brother, began to shiver and couldn't feel his feet; he'd only brought lightweight "cabin" layers. With the rules that governed my family's usual interactions blown away in the breeze, three headstrong personalities turned to me—the backpacker—to unite them. I quickly triaged their fatigue and warmth and turned four individuals into a team. First, I dispatched my brother to run to the cabin to start the fire I knew we'd need.

> Credit: istockphoto

My mom, dad, and I pushed on until my dad's muttering turned toward delirium. He wanted to stay with the group, but I knew by sticking around he'd become a liability so I gave him a job, too: push ahead and widen the track for me and Mom.

As building a snow shelter became a real consideration, I thought about digging a snow trench, but I decided our limited energy was best spent on getting to the fully stocked cabin. Meanwhile, my mom's pace had slowed to about 200 yards an hour. Could I rig my avalanche shovel to pull her? Nope. Could I carry her? Deep breath. In 50- to 100-yard stretches, I shuttled the packs ahead and then ran back and carried my mom the same distance. I strained to hold onto her legs through thick gloves, shuffling along the path broken by the others.

I pretended like it was easy as I grunted out involved questions to distract her from the pain. But she distracted me, too, by telling jokes and old stories and marveling at how quiet and special snow-cloaked woods could be in the dead of night. A survival epic was going on, but she either didn't notice or knew basking in the fear wouldn't make a difference anyway. Her chatter kept me going. I repeated the haul-packs-then-haul-mom process until we finally saw a glow through the trees. The cabin. It was 11 p.m.

Inside, Jeff and my dad huddled by the roaring stove, telling tales of hallucinations, wrong turns, swooping owls. I collapsed to the carpet. My refreshed mom had the reserves to keep the fire going and spirits high. Soon, we were thawed and self-medicating with a Malbec slushy. But only because of our teamwork in getting to shelter: brother's speed to the fire, Dad's dogged trailblazing, my donkey endurance, Mom's unflappable good humor. It all got us pulling in the same direction, ensuring that this is a story we get to keep telling around the winter fire every New Year's Eve.

// GIMME SHELTER: BUILDING WILDERNESS SHELTERS

Shelter is the often the thin margin keeping you and death distant acquaintances in the wild. It's the first line of defense, the place you build your life-giving fire, the temporary home where you shore up the mental strength you'll need to conquer any ordeal. If you're losing daylight and don't have a tent, it's easy for fear to descend with the temperature and the light. Don't panic: These tested shelter-making techniques will help you survive the night.

Basic: Clothing

It may not be the most obvious when thinking of shelter, but your primary shelter is clothing, so play it safe on excursions from camp and take a jacket and hat. On every trip, pack a synthetic or wool next-to-skin layer, an insulating middle layer, and a waterproof exterior shell jacket.

➤ *Shelter is the first line of defense.* Credit: istockphoto

Good: Fashion a Bed of Leaves

You lose heat to the ground and the air, so you want insulation both above and below. Look for piles of dry foliage, needles, and moss at the base of a tree, and scoop out a trough for your body, or make a heap the size of a single-bed mattress. Collect a stack of cover-up material nearby. Gather three to five times what you think you'll need; the nest will compress, and adding significant warmth requires about two feet of insulation both above and below your body. Lie in your pile, and cover up with your collected debris.

It's easy and warm—with ample supplies, you can be covered in ten minutes—but don't expect much deep sleep with all the pokey sticks and creepy-crawly bedmates. Though it stays remarkably dry during drizzles, it will soak through in direct rain. Situate your bed of leaves under tree cover.

Pro tip: Wind and anxious tossing can quickly scatter your maple duvet. Build in the lee of wind-blocking features. Orient for southern or eastern exposure, which will be warmer.

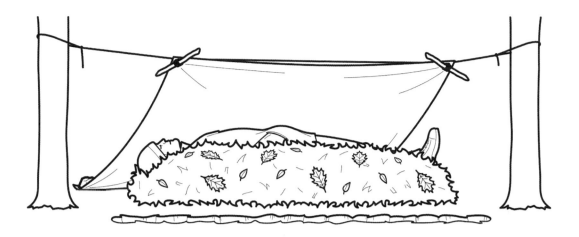

Better: Build a Tarp Shelter

Use paracord (a woven nylon cord about the width of a shoelace but much stronger; it's available in many lengths at most hardware and outdoor stores and Amazon) and stick toggles to secure grommets along your tarp's edge. String the tarp tightly between two trees at waist height. Angle and secure the loose side flush to the ground with rocks or by staking with sticks; it will be angled and open on the other side. Fill the back and base with insulating leaves (see illustration).

Conserving calories in a survival situation is critical, and this shelter goes up in minutes with few supplies. However, wind can catch your tarp if it's gusty or you set up in unprotected areas; build behind windbreaks and so the open side faces away from the wind, or secure the top low to the ground for a shorter profile. **Pro tip:** When it's cold, build a trench fire paralleling the length of the open side of your tarp (within 5 feet for optimal heat); angle the rocks on the fire's far side to reflect warmth toward you.

HACK THIS: STICK TOGGLE

Create a taut shelter and save rope with this simple fastener. First, find finger-width, 3-inch-long sticks—the toggles. Thread your line into a grommet, wrap it around one toggle three times, and thread back through the hole.

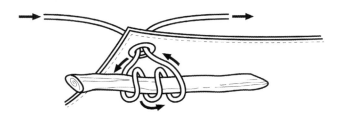

Best: Improvise an A-frame

Find a strong, navel-high tree limb growing roughly parallel to the ground, or sloping toward it, to use as a ridgepole—or make one yourself by placing a branch atop a stump, an overhanging boulder, or in a tree notch (see illustration). Lean branches against the limb on both sides, creating an A-frame that's just wide enough for your body. Make the walls thick and angled to shed water and provide insulation. Continue piling sticks and debris until no light penetrates. Fill the inside with insulating leaves and foliage.

In my testing, this shelter was the warmest and sturdiest when conditions were cold and windy. It held heat and offered protection from moderate precip (you'll need to add a plastic layer to repel full-on downpours). The only downside: Building it takes time and energy (a few hours, if supplies are nearby). But if you're in a branch-littered forest, uninjured, and hydrated while awaiting rescue, the comfort is worth the extra effort.

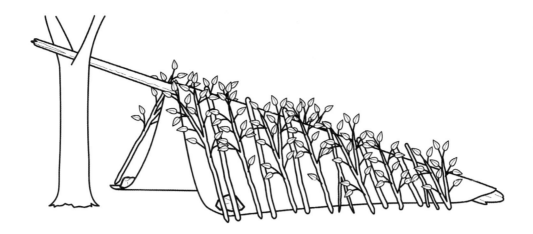

Pro tip: Have a garbage bag? You should. Cut it open and place it between layers of the roof's material to add low-tech waterproofing. Got two? Make a door to block wind.

How to Scout a Safe Shelter Spot

Save energy and stay more comfortable by exploiting natural features. If you get lucky and find a cave, you might not have to build a shelter at all.

1. **Look for existing shelters first.** Hollow logs, tree wells, and rock crevices may provide quick protection for a fraction of the calories you'd spend

HACK THIS: PLASTIC IS FANTASTIC

Use man-made materials whenever possible. "It's much easier and quicker to build a lean-to with a space blanket or a tube tent with trash bags hung over a rope than with debris," says survival superstar Cody Lundin. The reflective side of a space blanket will divert the sun's rays in the desert and retain body heat in cold conditions.

cobbling together a shelter. Blowdowns, or trees with dense, low canopies work, too.

2. **Look for depressions** at the bases of healthy evergreens; overhanging boughs shed precipitation.

3. **Avoid natural cold sinks.** Construct your shelter above low features like ravines and valley bottoms, where cold air settles. Also stay away from wind-exposed areas.

4. Need a fire to stay warm? **Build in level, well-drained spots** near wide rock faces or overhanging boulders, which will bounce heat back at you. Be careful around overhanging cliffs—heat can loosen rocks.

➤ *Even if you have shelter, building walls out of insulating snow can help add protection.* Credit: istockphoto

// HOME BUYER: ULTRALIGHT BIVY SACKS

Why build a shelter when you can carry one in your jacket pocket? The bivouac has a long history. Soldiers used it to improvise safety in enemy territory; climbers and adventurers use it for fast-and-light shelter in places where humans rarely tread. A bivy sack can keep you safe and feel like home sans tent or anything else. All of the models below will easily fit in a dayhiker's pack. Voilà: instant shelter.

Burliest

You'll sleep like a baby—with and without a sleeping bag—after unpacking Rab's Survival Zone (8 ounces; rab.equipment/us/) from its eggplant-size stuff sack. The Pertex Shield waterproof/breathable shell impressed: One tester, sweat-soaked after a night hike, expected to shiver in a tree hollow when temps in the area dropped to 50°F, but after ten minutes of venting, he stayed dry through an all-night drizzle.

Minimalist

Terra Nova's Moonlite (7 ounces; terra-nova.co.uk) is made of superlight micro ripstop nylon (be gentle!) that compresses to the size of an orange, and the

HACK THIS: HACKING THE FOREST

Building a shelter with natural materials doesn't always comply with Leave No Trace ethics. Practice these techniques in your own backyard, but only gather boughs, branches, mosses, and leaves in the backcountry if you're in a true crisis. Even then, try to use dead or downed wood—not only will you preserve the forest, you'll save crucial energy by not hacking at limbs on live trees.

waterproof/breathable membrane keeps you comfortable on cool nights. Fave feature: the easy-to-use drawstring. Drawback: a narrow cut that could compress bag loft and crowd broad-shouldered campers.

Bargain

Essentially an emergency blanket welded into a tube, the SOL Emergency Bivvy (3.8 ounces; adventuremedicalkits.com) employs an aluminized coating that reflects body heat, adding 10°F of warmth. However, the crinkly fabric doesn't breathe, so prepare for a clammy sleep. It packs down to the size of a tennis ball and it's inexpensive, which makes it a no-brainer backup for day hikers.

➤ *Man-made materials can give you an advantage in staying dry and warm.* Credit: istockphoto

// WINTER IS COMING: SNOW SHELTERS

If you're caught in a raging blizzard, fast shelter is key to survival. Luckily, snow is a fantastic insulator: Even when the temperature hits the negatives, with a few (living) bodies inside these shelters temperatures can climb well above freezing. Master a few simple techniques and you can weave magic to keep your party warm with little more than the building materials around you.

Build a Snow Cave

With practice, building snow caves can be reasonably fast and efficient—but the right consistency of snow and location is essential. Practice makes perfect, and teams are best: Snow caves usually take 3-4 hours to build.

1. **Find a large drift** where wind has driven and firmed up the snow. The texture should be the same as good snowball-making or snowman-making white stuff.
2. Start digging low to the ground and **keep the entrance low.** Needing to crawl or crouch to get in is a good thing.
3. Carefully begin hollowing out your snow cave, making sure there's enough space for your party, but **keep it a tight squeeze.** Walls should be about a foot to 18 inches thick to keep from collapsing.
4. Try to keep the interior bell-shaped for maximum structural integrity. **Pack the sides and ceiling** to keep it strong.
5. Use the snow you hollow out from your ceiling to **build a sleeping platform that is higher than the entrance.** That way, you'll avoid drafts and bask in the heat trapped in your snow cave.
6. Poke a 2-inch hole in the roof to **create ventilation. Use a stick or a treking pole.**

Build an Igloo

Igloos are amazingly warm and even fun to build once you've mastered the skill. They're eminently practical, too: They're just as warm as a snow cave, but have more interior light, and you stay drier making them. Experienced builders working with good snow can create an igloo in 30 or 40 minutes, but snow conditions are critical, and you'll want a team to mitigate the effort.

1. **You need deep, consolidated snow**—think squeaky like Styrofoam. And you'll need the right tools: a small shovel and a snow saw. (Create your own

➤ *Trust us: It's more comfortable than it looks.* Credit: istockphoto

packed snow: Stomp snow; pile more snow on top until it's several feet high; stomp as you go. Let it sit for two hours to solidify.)

2. Mark your circle and **pack it down for a stable platform.**

3. **Make snow bricks about 8 feet in diameter.** Cut blocks 6 inches wide, 18 inches tall, and 30 inches long. They should be of uniform size. Carve them slightly concave on the top, bottom, and sides, like "starved" rectangles. This causes the corners to seat against each other better. You'll want a partner, so one person can cut blocks and one can place them. The number of bricks you'll need depends on the size of your igloo, but it'll be almost certainly more than you think. For a small two-person igloo, stop with twenty, begin the following steps, and add on as needed.

4. **Make a door.** Lay two blocks on edge, pointing outward and slightly wider than shoulder-width apart. Lay a block across them to form a roof. Later, you'll dig the entryway deeper.

5. **Begin the dome** by laying blocks, on edge, in a climbing ramp/spiral pattern (stronger and easier to roof over than even layers of blocks). Shave the blocks' height to achieve the ramp effect. Offset corners of new blocks so they don't sit directly on top of those below. Tilt the blocks inward, more with each row; you want a 45-degree angle by row three.

6. Make sure the blocks' upper corners brace solidly against each other. Set each block with a shove. Once the walls get too high to step over, **dig out the door.** Close the hole in the top with a custom block, shaped like a bottle stopper.

7. **Finish the igloo** by packing snow over the gaps and cracks, poking vent holes through the roof, and smoothing the dome interior so that irregular points in the roof won't drip.

You probably carry one of these already (right?). Now, make the most of it with these seven life-saving techniques.

HEAT REFLECTOR

The classic crinkly survival blanket looks flimsy, but it's more versatile than the comfiest duvet. Here are a few tricks to get the most out of yours. Quick heat: Sit a comfortable distance from your fire, and pull the blanket (shiny side facing the flame) up above your head to create a pocket. All-night comfort: Line the ceiling of your emergency A-frame shelter or tie up in lean-to fashion (peak height 3 to 4 feet) next to any heat source to reflect radiating warmth (including your body heat) back toward you.

SUNSHADE

Rig just like the heat reflector, but with the shiny side facing out. Bonus: Reflected light creates a rescue signal for overhead aircraft. —Tony Nester, Ancient Pathways Survival School

HEAT SACK

Burrito yourself or a hypothermic buddy in the blanket with the reflective edge facing in. First, wrap yourself or your buddy in warm layers and sleeping bags, then use the emergency blanket as the outermost layer to block wind and trap body heat. —Benjamin Pressley, author *Can You Survive?*

PASSIVE SIGNALING

Cut the space blanket into short strips and tie the strips onto tree branches, bushes, or weeds. They can catch sunlight and alert rescuers to your position. —Tim MacWelch, Advanced Survival Training School

HARVEST RAIN

Dig a hole, line it with the blanket, and wait for rain. No ability to dig? Tie it taut by all four corners and put a rock at its center to create a low point where water can collect. —Tim MacWelch

MELT SNOW

Lay the blanket on the snow, then press a small concavity 2 feet wide and a foot deep in the center of the blanket. Sprinkle small amounts of snow around the rim. Heat from the sun will hit the snow directly and by reflection,

> Credit: Caveman Collective

melting it into drinking water. —Tom Brown Jr., Tom Brown Jr.'s Tracker School

PRESERVE FOOD

Build a simple backcountry meat smoker. Start by making a 5-foot-tall tripod out of 1-inch-thick sticks. Construct a triangular platform halfway up by lashing a stick between each tripod leg—your meat will hang from these. Cover with your survival blanket, leaving an opening at the bottom to tend your fire. Build a smoky fire with hardwoods, and regulate the airflow to keep the wood smoldering (not burning). Meat smoked overnight lasts a week. —Kellie Nightlinger, Wild Woman Outdoors

// TEMP JOB: READ THE WEATHER

If shelter is all about protection from the elements, understanding the language of clouds goes a long way toward determining conditions, danger, and proper responses to those elements. But you don't need a degree in meteorology: Learn to identify three families of clouds, and you'll be able to forecast rain, sun, and deadly storms.

Cumulonimbus Clouds

How they form: When the sun heats up a moist air mass, or when a cold front wedges underneath it, that mass can rise violently upward—think afternoon

> *Nimbostratus clouds mean prolonged periods of cloud or moderate rain.* Credit: istockphoto

> *Cumulus clouds point to bluebird skies and calm weather.* Credit: istockphoto

thermals rising over the Rockies or a low-pressure front rolling into the Smokies. As the air rises, its water vapor condenses, lifting the cloud even higher. The result: massive thunderclouds piled miles high.

What to expect: Cumulonimbus clouds can develop in as few as twenty minutes. The faster, taller, and darker they build up, the faster and more violent the energy release. Translation: fierce downpours, wind, lightning, and hail. In North America, thunderstorms are most common over the Florida peninsula and Colorado's southeastern plains, but they also form commonly on the windward side of mountain ranges, above unevenly heated terrain, and wherever two air masses collide.

Warning signs: Watch for altocumulus (midlevel, puffy clouds), especially in warm weather. These typically signal a cold front, and once it collides with warm air, afternoon thunderstorms might result.

What to do: Cut short your outing, descending from high points or jagged terrain and avoiding tall, isolated objects, like lone trees. If there's lightning, move 50 feet away from others, and squat on top of insulating material with your head down, feet together, and arms wrapped around your legs. This isn't any safer in a direct strike, but in the event of a nearby ground strike, it minimizes points of contact. Basically, don't end up in this position in the first place.

➤ *Cumulonimbus clouds presage thunderstorms and potentially chaotic weather.* Credit: istockphoto

Nimbostratus Clouds

How they form: These sheets of gray and white blanket the sky—the quintessential cloudy day (the word stratus is actually Latin for "layer"). They form when a relatively stable air mass (not very different in temperature from the air around it) condenses above cooler air.

What to expect: It can point to steady and moderate precipitation—or just more cloudy days, since much of the precipitation will evaporate before it hits the ground. The lower, thicker, and darker the cloud, the sooner the precipitation.

➤ *In most places, high and wispy cirrus clouds mean good weather.* Credit: istockphoto

Warning signs: First, high, faint cirrostratus clouds create a haze across the sky and a halo around the sun, hinting at rain or snow within twenty-four hours. The cirrostratus clouds might then lower and thicken into altostratus clouds, obscuring the sun's exact location and suggesting continuous precipitation within twelve hours. If the altostratus clouds descend farther, they become dark nimbostratus clouds, which entirely obscure the sun and often produce steady precipitation that can last hours or days.

What to do: Gauge if you need to bust out miles to reach a campsite or cross slick terrain (say, a scree field) before the interminable drizzle.

Cirrus Clouds

How they form: Found more than 20,000 feet high, these curly, wispy clouds consist of ice crystals and can form in any season. Cirrus generally appear white but, at dawn and dusk, can take on a rainbow of colors.

What to expect: Cirrus clouds suggest fair weather.

Warning signs: Don't confuse cirrus clouds with other high-altitude clouds such as cirrostratus clouds or high, lumpy cirrocumulus clouds. The former signal a good chance of rain or snow within twenty-four hours, and the latter often indicate cold weather; in the tropics, however, cirrocumulus clouds might mark a hurricane's approach.

What to do: Milk the weather window—enjoy a long lunch or tack on another objective.

SURVIVING SIX DAYS ON A LEDGE

BY DAVID CICOTELLO AS TOLD TO JOSH PRESTIN

// THERE WAS NO ESCAPE: LOUIS WAS DEAD OR DYING, AND I COULD NOT GET TO HIM.

I watched my big brother, Louis, smear out of sight and over the edge of a 100-foot exit rappel from No Mans Canyon, and listened for his confirmation of a safe landing. Instead, I heard, "Oops. The rope is too short." Then he said, "No biggie." He's my older brother, I thought. He always has things under control. Just then the rope whizzed through the sling that was securing it and was gone.

I screamed Louis's name into the afternoon calm. I held my breath, hoping for something, anything, to let me know he was OK. Silence. My voice grew hoarse and thin in that canyon as I paced a ledge in the snaking, trough-like exit slot looking for a way down. But there was no escape: Louis was dead or dying, and I could not get to him.

Breathe, I told myself. I ran my fingers along the sandstone, looking for handholds leading back the way we'd come. All of them crumbled or ran out. For two hours I tried to get flesh to stick to rock. On my final try, I fell. It wasn't far, but it was a wake-up call. I could die trying to get out of here.

I regrouped. I knew I had to survive at least five days—until Friday, when our families back in Tennessee would miss our check-in call and send help. I inventoried my day pack (we were base camping): turkey sandwich, energy bar, orange, and a bag of cashews; a liter of tea with half a lemon, 15 ounces of water; a knife, some matches, climbing webbing, 25 feet of static rope, a harness, several carabiners, and a rudimentary med kit.

might end up like him. I carved my name and a single hash mark—for day one—into the gritty sandstone.

Rain came the second night. I was awake when it started, shivering in the near-freezing night. I curled deeper into the fetal position and forced myself to sing "America the Beautiful" and "Amazing Grace" to ward off despair. The cold nipped harder at my fingers and toes with each passing hour.

As Wednesday became Thursday, I started to fear that rescue wouldn't come. The lemon had gone rancid in my tea, and I couldn't get it out. My lips were parched because I only allowed myself tiny rations of water. My clothing sagged off my frame. I needed a contingency plan. I tied webbing pieces and my static rope together and tossed the line down over the edge—hoping it would hit some rock structure I couldn't see, a possible way out. Twice I did this, and twice, nothing. It was like being trapped all over again.

Out of Sight, Out of Options

Friday brought the fifth hash mark next to my name. I could hardly make spit in my mouth. When I sat still the only sound I heard was my stomach's growl. I was down to my last sip of water, but refused to drink it. I knew I should have, but I couldn't bear the thought of being without something to drink.

The sun had already set when I heard the chopper. Without time to build a fire, I stood waving my "HELP" sign and shouting, but my efforts couldn't escape the canyon's dark and din. Hearing that sound fade into nothingness sank me lower than at any previous point. I slept. Late Saturday morning the helicopter returned. They'd seen my brother's body below, and this time they saw me, too. I downed my last sip of water in celebration and readied myself for a somber trip out. I was joyous to be rescued, but it was a joy unfulfilled. I left a lot in that canyon.

As sun washed the canyon's bulbous walls in muted pinks and warm reds, I found a small, flat perch where I could sleep. It was 4 feet above the slot canyon's true floor and set back from the course of potential floods. I cut the padding from my pack and used it as a mat to insulate my core against the chill. That night, I watched the stars pass between towering canyon walls. I thought about my brother.

Then the Rains Came

The next morning, I woke into the same nightmare. I did little things—gathered flood-deposited twigs for comfort fires, cut away my pack's frame sheet and arranged webbing on it to spell "HELP"—because if my mind wasn't engaged in some task, my thoughts would creep to my brother below and the possibility that I

➤ Credit: istockphoto

FIRE | 2

othing rekindles our primal connection to the open flame like a backcountry campfire. It's more than Caveman TV: We instinctively understand it's the one killer application against inexorable, creeping death. Whether it's encroaching cold or stalking predators, if you can build a fire, you can live to starve, shiver, run, or fight another day.

Lucky adventurers often learn this truth after happenstance plays a quick, cruel joke on them by flooding a tent or forcing a too-long ski tour. Blue lips and trembling fingers recover fast in a hut with a blazing stove or when clutching a hot toddy in a toasty, packed, trail-town bar after an aborted trip. But sometimes we learn it at the sharp end, when nothing else will keep us alive. That's how I learned it with my brother in Wyoming's Wind River Range, as dumb beginner hikers clad in all-cotton on a sweaty death march to get to the Cirque of the Towers and back in one foolhardy October day.

We should've seen the signs. Midway through our 17-mile trip, our spreading sweat stains stung us in the shade of the imposing granite spires when the wind blew. We should've taken the frozen elk carcass under the blue glass of Big Sandy Lake as an omen to turn back. But the warmth of a high-altitude sun on our faces and our fast pace to the cirque lulled us into a false sense of security. The sun dropped all too soon behind the serrated skyline, and the sky was still orange when the shivering spread from our fingers and ears to our necks and chests. By the time we stumbled into the Big Sandy campground, we were babbling inanities and hallucinating cougars behind every trunk. We would've been an easy, incoherent dinner if the visions turned real.

We huddled together in our Jeep, burning gas and the heater, but we were unable to keep our legs from shaking like Elvis's. Wet cotton bled heat from our cores. The headlights illuminated several massive stumps ringing the nearest campfire. With a dearth of firewood around and no campers nearby, we rolled the makeshift stools into the fire ring, shoved newspapers and a cardboard Pabst Blue Ribbon case scrounged from underneath the car and lit the damn thing, hoping for the best. I'm sure other sacrifices went into the fire to keep it alive. Maybe maps, maybe newspapers, possibly car registrations. We were so addled that even today neither my brother nor I can remember what we burned. High winds and luck turned it into a crackling, 5-foot-tall ziggurat of burning pine. In twenty minutes, our senses and core temps stabilized enough for us to realize how idiotically close to calamity we had come.

➤ Credit: istockphoto

Admittedly, that incident nurtured a lifelong interest in setting things ablaze into a sort of purposeful pyromania. A fire lust that flowered in adolescence by tipping arrows with acetone or bottle rockets and using microwaves to interrogate tight-lipped G.I. Joes became cloaked in the responsibility and language of backcountry survival. I've made punky torches to keep mosquitoes away; my fire-starting potions and experiments include flint, Fritos, Vaseline, olive oil, alcohol, feather sticks, Wet Ones, magnifying lenses, and batteries.

So yes: Setting shit on fire is a whole lot of fun. But knowing you can save someone's life or your own by doing it is even sweeter.

➤ *Fire rings help keep your fire under control and safe.* Credit: istockphoto

// SITING YOUR FIRE: LOCATION, LOCATION, LOCATION

From the dawn of history to dusk last night, fire is humankind's oldest and most useful tool. Learning to harness its strength to cook, stay warm, and provide light will do more than help you survive—it'll connect you to a primal force as old and powerful as time itself. The first step toward success is determining where to build your blaze. Environmental placement is paramount: Wind can be a massive help or a massive hindrance. Some spots that don't seem wet (like a dry ditch) will actually hold fire-inhibiting moisture just below the surface.

Most important of all is control: Whether you need a life-saving bonfire or cooking coals, it's important to use location to keep fire under your direction. Remember, there's a saying for when an idea proliferates really fast: "It spread like wildfire." Remember that, and follow local fire regulations to keep yourself safe.

How to Prep a Suitable Area for Your Fire

Like many survival skills, planning and preparation before action is the first and best hack. Starting a fire in a less-than-desirable spot can significantly hinder your ability to start it, keep it alive, or keep it under control. Desperate situations might goad you into burning something—anything—before cold or weather sets in. Don't. Take a deep breath, and do the following.

1. **Choose a sheltered spot** beneath an opening in the tree canopy or where limbs are at least 12 feet high. Sheltered locations, like against a rock face or in a grove of trees, will help you stay dry and warm.
2. If the ground is already dirt or sand, clear away any flammable debris in a 5-foot circle. If the ground is grassy or thick with duff, lay down a tarp or space blanket (folded to the size of your fire).
3. **Collect** loose dirt, sand, or gravel and stones.

4. **Build a circular, flat mound** 3 to 5 inches thick and as wide as a car tire on the cleared ground or your tarp. This protects against leaving behind a burn mark or letting embers spread. Never site a fire in a ditch, which will hinder the flames' ability to draw in air at the base.

5. In gusty weather, **dig a pit** for your fire to sit in—the stronger the wind, the deeper your pit should be.

6. Use fist-size or larger stones to build a fire ring, forming a physical barrier.

7. **Have a few liters of water handy** to use for emergency extinguishment.

// FUEL: PICKUP STICKS

Once you've found a safe, sheltered place to build your fire, you'll need to feed it. But not all fuels are created equally: Newspaper gets a fire going but dies quickly; large logs are all but impossible to light with a match alone, but burn for hours once lit.

HACK THIS: IT'S WINDY

Wind makes fires hard to start and control. Site your fire on the lee side of a natural windbreak, like a large boulder or fallen stump. If it's slightly breezy, protect your nascent flame with a cupped hand or your body or pack. If the wind is blowing up to 10 mph (saplings are swaying), drive an inch-thick green stick into the ground at a 30-degree angle. Point the end of the stick with the wind, and place your tinder where the stick meets the ground. Lean kindling onto the angled stick, creating walls. In wind faster than 10 mph, forgo the fire unless it's an emergency.

➤ *Gather kindling to help start your fire.* Credit: istockphoto

The right fuel makes all the difference. You'll need the right combination and amount of logs, sticks, kindling, and fuel to make a fire and make it last. Learning how to identify the right kinds, getting enough, and getting organized can be the difference between life and death.

How to Prep for a Successful Blaze

Here's a common nightmare: With cold weather and darkness closing in, you finally see light and feel heat from the nascent embers of your fire . . . only to watch them twinkle out when you run out kindling, or snuff them with a too-big stick. You can avoid this tragic scenario by getting organized. Gather the following types of fuel, and organize them in neat piles next to you and your fire. Spend your time foraging in daylight so you don't have to go sprinting off into the dark just because you ran out of tiny sticks. Another solid rule of thumb: Gather thrice what you need—especially when it comes to the large, long-burning fuel that'll keep you warm through an entire night.

Here's how to prep for a successful blaze when you're far from a pre-prepped cabin stove or gas station bundle of logs.

TINDER

This fine, flammable material easily takes a tiny spark or flame, and accelerates and spreads it. Many hikers bring tinder from home, but if you're foraging for it (see our Tinder Finder on page 40), nab at least a handful.

HACK THIS: SIGNAL FIRES

One of the best ways to get found in a survival situation is with a signal fire. Fires in high locations are more likely to get attention. Try setting three fires in a triangle—the geometric shape stands out from the tangle of wilderness, and three is an international symbol for help. Adding unnatural materials to a fire often makes black smoke. To get excess smoke, add evergreen boughs, soggy logs, and wet leaves.

KINDLING

Gather enough finger-thick sticks that you need two hands to hold it all. Kindling transitions your fire from a flicker to a roaring blaze and quickly creates coals, which raises the temperature and brings wood closer to its combustion point. Your fire isn't assured until you start seeing coals. Pine and other softwoods (such as cedar, spruce, and aspen) light fastest. Pinecones can add a flammable punch.

THIN FUEL

Thumb- to 1-inch-thick wood is best for perking up the fire if it begins to wane, and for producing good cooking coals. Collect about three times as much fuel wood as kindling for forty-five minutes of fire.

WRIST-THICK WOOD

Look for slow-burning hardwoods (such as oak, hickory, ash, and birch), which will throw out heat for hours.

BIG LOGS

Downed behemoths combust for hours, rarely burn completely, and are difficult to extinguish; skip them except in survival situations.

5 RULES FOR FORAGING FIREWOOD

Follow these tips for a crackling, low-impact fire. In a survival situation, low-impact goes out the window.

1. Look for dry wood with little or loose bark. A good, seasoned piece will give a sharp crack when snapped.
2. Collect a diversity of wood types. Softwoods (like pine) ignite easily but burn out fast. Hardwoods (like oak) produce better coals for cooking and are a good bet for a long fire.
3. Allow time to search far and wide. Scavenge for deadfall away from camp to minimize environmental impacts.
4. Get enough so you're not hunting for wood in the dark. An armful of wood equals forty-five minutes of fire.
5. Burn nothing thicker than an adult's wrist. To break a big branch, wedge one end in a forked tree and lever it toward you until the piece snaps.

HACK THIS: I CAN'T FIND DRY WOOD

Look for dead twigs, branches, or boughs high and dry. Wood snagged in the forest canopy will be drier than stuff resting on the ground with the damp leaves and soil. If there's snow on the ground, stamp down a 4-foot-square area. Next, build a square platform of green logs, arranged flat, to keep the fire off the wet surface and prevent it from sinking.

If it's raining hard, you might think you're SOL. Not so: If you didn't bring your own tinder, scavenge for dry grass or bark near the roots of downed trees, which act as a weather shield. Find a large piece of bark (dry on the inside) to use as a platform to keep the wood off the wet ground. If you can set up beneath a tree without risking setting it ablaze, do it. Otherwise, lay a large piece of bark across your fire pit to shield your nascent flame.

PREP YOUR WOOD

Break all your collected wood into uniform 12- to 18-inch sections. Do this away from your campfire to avoid hitting others. Arrange sticks by size and keep them close at hand, so you don't have to hunt around or divert your attention from your fledgling flame.

➤ *Natural material can be found anywhere to turn into tinder.* Credit: istockphoto

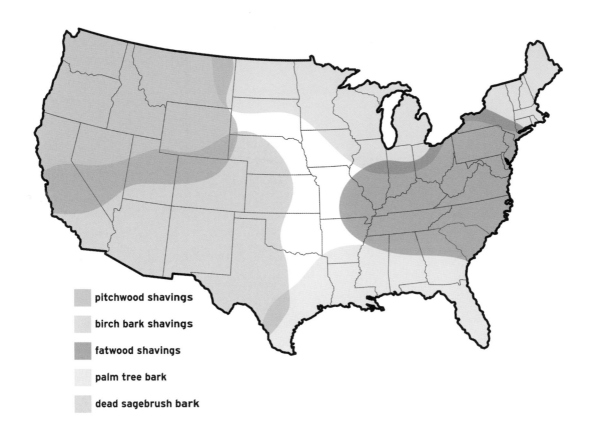

pitchwood shavings

birch bark shavings

fatwood shavings

palm tree bark

dead sagebrush bark

Tinder Finder

If there's anything to know about the plant biome of North America, it's that a lot of it is flammable. No matter where you are, there's natural material for the taking to get your tinder. Familiarize yourself with these common sources.

■ WESTERN STATES

Find pitch wood, an orange- to red-colored wood, at the base of dead branches on yellow pine trees (ponderosa and lodgepole, Western larch, and Douglas fir). Use your knife to create shavings. They'll burn in the rain.

■ NORTHERN STATES

The oils in birch bark, an easy-to-identify bark, are highly flammable, even when wet. Remove or forage bark, and use your knife to scrape a pile of fine shavings.

■ SOUTHWEST / PLAINS

Scrap dead sagebrush bark into a pile and then rub it between your hands to fluff it up.

■ GULF COAST / SOUTH ATLANTIC

Palm tree bark is a fluffy, fibrous bark found at the base of the palm frond (branch) and makes exceptional tinder, but watch out for spiders!

■ MID-ATLANTIC / SOUTH

Fatwood (pitch wood by a different name) is found here in longleaf, pitch, and loblolly pines.

EVERYWHERE

Here is some tinder you can find everywhere.

- ➤ Dead, dry leaves and grasses: Gather and arrange loosely.
- ➤ Conifer needles: Target pine, spruce, cedar, cypress, larch, and hemlock. Look for ones that are attached to the node.
- ➤ Inner bark: Scrape or shred into a pile and then rub together with your hands to fluff it up. Best bets: cedar, mulberry, juniper, aspen, cottonwood, black and yellow poplar, and oak.
- ➤ Wood shavings: Look for dead, dry branches under trees or use your knife to whittle away wet layers.
- ➤ Cattail fluff: This "flash tinder" goes up quickly; have slower-burning tinder handy. Collect it in marshy and grassy areas from late summer to early spring.
- ➤ Dandelion fluff: Find it in the spring and early fall. Like cattail fluff, this stuff goes up fast.

HACK THIS: NO NATURAL SOURCES

Let's say you can't find natural materials for tinder, or it's too dark to look. Never fear! You can scrounge man-made tinder from inside your pack. Here's a handy guide.

BURN THIS . . .

- Alcohol-based hand sanitizer: A grape-size dab will burn almost invisibly for ninety seconds.
- White gas: Though it evaporates in the open air, it does so slowly.
- Cooking oil: Unrefined oils work best.
- DEET bug sprays: Burning sprays might create some unhealthy fumes, but you might take the risk if you need a fire in an emergency and it's all you have.
- Gauze bandages: These are good for burning, as are paper products, like toilet paper, tissues, trash, or playing cards.
- Steel wool: It even lights when wet!
- Fabric: Apply the above fire accelerants to cotton or wool garments, or nylon. Torn strips of cotton ignite easily and blaze brightly. Tighter weaves burn longer, so shirts and underwear work better than socks, for example.

DON'T BURN . . .

- Butane from an opened lighter: When exposed to air, it evaporates quickly.
- Polyester synthetics: These ignite slowly and melt into a fire-killing plastic residue.

Light 'Em Up: Homemade Fire-Starters, Tested

From Vaseline-soaked cotton balls to grandpa's hand-carved feather stick, we've heard of just about anything being turned into a reliable fire-starter. And it's a time-honored tradition for outdoorsmen to pass on these secret homemade fire-starters like heirlooms to the next generation of bush kids. But which of them work best? We've tested every fuel source under the sun to figure out which surprising fuels start a fire every time. Here are a few that work best.

➤ *Cashews make for great fuel.* Credit: istockphoto

COTTON BALL

I soaked this classic in olive oil, Vaseline, and hand sanitizer. Olive oil burns longest, but alcohol is easiest to light. Solution? Use both: Soak it in the oil and add a dab of hand sanitizer as an accelerant for nearly nine minutes of fire. Thirty seconds under a lighter gets it going in a downpour.

Difficulty: Medium

FRITO

This tasty, salty treat comes packed with enough oils to light and burn for nearly two minutes—even after being dunked in a stream. **Pro tip:** The increased surface area of a Tostito buys you another minute of flame—and two more minutes of thin, red-hot coals after it gutters out.

Difficulty: Easy

CASHEW

This trail-mix staple is tough to light (especially when wet), but after I attempted to light a single raw nut for 45 seconds, it caught and yielded 2 minutes and 40 seconds of 1-inch-high flames—more than enough to light a golf ball-size tinder nest. Almonds and peanuts also work, but cashews burn best.

Difficulty: Hard

SOL TINDER-QUIK

An earplug-size knot of über-flammable Tinder-Quik fiber (surviveoutdoorslonger .com) survived downpours, dunkings, and dirt/debris to burn for 3 minutes and 18 seconds in our test (a dime-size coal glows for another 1 minute 30 seconds). Bonus: Tinder-Quik lights with just a few sparks.

Difficulty: Easy

➤ Credit: istockphoto

Advanced Pyrotechnics: Make the Ultimate Fire-Starter

Confession: I'm a bit of a pyromaniac. I've spent unhealthy amounts of time experimenting with all kinds of material to see what burns best, longest, and fastest. Out of everything I've tried, a secret shared to me by a crusty camp host deep in the Olympic rainforest remains my favorite—I've used the materials he told me about to get fires going in a downpour. Make your fire faster and more reliably with this never-fail firebomb made from a cardboard egg carton, dryer lint, dental floss, and a candle.

1. **Gather materials:** Collect dryer lint, cut the cardboard egg carton into a dozen individual cups (no Styrofoam!), and chop or smash a candle into small, easy-to-melt pieces. (Unscented is best, but maybe you love loganberry.) Cut the floss into 12-inch-long pieces. Fill a small pot with a few inches of water, and place it on the stove. Find a mason jar.

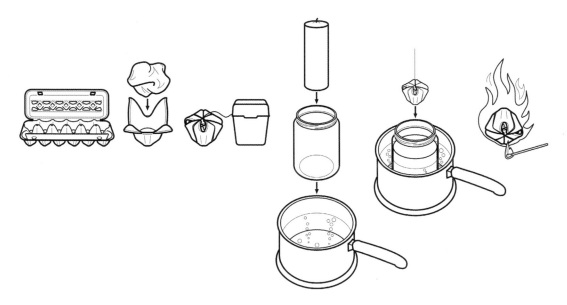

2. **Stuff each egg cup** full with dryer lint and fold over the edges to close it. Tie it shut with a foot-long length of floss; each cup should have a 6- to 10-inch floss tail you can grasp it by.

3. Meanwhile, **boil the pot of water** on the stove. Fill the mason jar with chopped wax, and using tongs, place the jar in the boiling water. Make sure the water can't get inside the jar. (You may need to steady the jar with tongs.)

4. Once the wax is completely melted, **dip each of your egg cups in the wax,** covering it completely and generously to waterproof it.

5. **Let the cups dry** for several hours.

6. Voila! Waterproof firebombs. When lit, the fire-starter emits a foot-tall flame for about eighteen minutes, even in the rain. Even wet tinder dries out with that much heat.

// ARCHITECTURE: BUILD IT UP, BURN IT DOWN

Plenty of survivors in extreme situations have gotten a fire going by simply tossing their fuels in a pile, lighting them, and hoping for the best. But that's the exception, because when a fire is really needed for survival, the conditions will likely be wet and cold, making fire starting and maintaining hard. When you build your fire,

➤ *Get your fire to burn, burn, burn.* Credit: istockphoto

some care and attention at the outset can go a long way to ensuring it lights and stays burning. A sustainable fire is crucial if you're stuck for a long time or if you've escaped the scary penumbra of hypothermia and don't particularly want to go back.

There are three classic modes of constructing your starter structure: teepee, lean-to, and log cabin. Which one is the best? It depends entirely on local conditions, materials, and experience. The constant is good airflow. For all of them, dig a shallow X under your kindling to boost ventilation. Otherwise, experiment with these three techniques to find which you prefer—or better yet, master all three.

Three Fire-Building Techniques

When it comes to staging your fire, there is no one right way to do it. Your best choice may depend on materials at hand, weather, location, and time. My advice? Experiment with each of them until you sear them all into your muscle memory.

TEEPEE

This technique is the top choice of *BACKPACKER* and experts. It's easy to make and produces tall flames quickly.

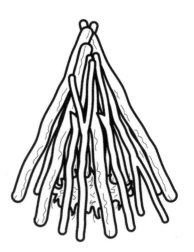

1. **Drive a forked, finger-thick stick into the ground** at a 45-degree angle over your tinder pile. Lean another same-width stick into the crook of the forked end.
2. **Add slightly thinner sticks,** maintaining a balanced structure by adding like-size pieces at the same time on either side of your teepee.
3. **Leave an opening** all the way to the center on the lee side so you can deliver a spark or flame to your tinder pile.
4. After lighting, **add more kindling** to the outside of the teepee. When a good bed of coals forms, add fuel, starting small so as not to smother your flame.

LOG CABIN

Damp logs, slightly green wood, and harder-to-ignite hardwoods dry in place with this technique.

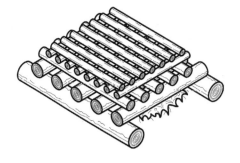

1. **Place 1-inch-thick pieces of fuel wood** on either side of your tinder pile, parallel to each other.
2. **The next layer of fuel wood should be slightly thinner** (thumb-thick), placed across the bottom two to form a square base (think Lincoln Logs).
3. Starting with the third layer, **place thin, well-spaced pieces of kindling flat** across the center. Starting here leaves space to insert your match.
4. **Continue with this overlaying pattern** until you've made a square structure about seven levels tall.

LEAN-TO

If you can't split larger logs, or it's slim pickings for smaller fuel wood, choose this fire design, which gets a log burning fast.

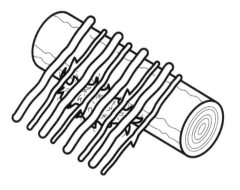

1. **Lay an arm-thick log in your fire area.** This is the support and windbreak. Put your tinder pile directly beside the log and on the lee side, if there is any wind.
2. **Lean kindling and thin fuel wood against the log** at a right angle, directly over the tinder pile.
3. Alternate between thin and thick pieces for easier fire uptake, and make sure to **leave plenty of space between sticks** so the fire can breathe.
4. To light, **reach under the lean-to with your match** or lighter.

3 RULES FOR HEALTHY FIRES

1. Ensure side flow: When combustion happens, surrounding air heats up and rises. Air rushes in from the sides to take its place, pushing equally from each direction; it's why flames lick upward instead of any other direction. Leave ½- to ¾-inch of space between kindling sticks (more space for larger pieces).

2. Keep kindling dry: Use a slab of bark or a few green logs on the ground to protect your kindling from moisture.

3. Think small: This isn't a homecoming bonfire. Your fire doesn't need to be much more than a foot high: More than that and you're wasting resources and energy. Large, open flames are hard to control and maintain.

// LIGHT YOUR FIRE: TIME TO BURN

Before the advent of instant firestarters like butane or potassium chlorate and phosphate, we had to make do with flint, friction tools, and other primitive means.

Yes, they worked, but here's the truth: They all suck.

Don't get me wrong: There's great value in the sense of empowerment and self-reliance that comes from mastering a bow drill or flint and knife. Any true survivor should master these over time—especially because fuel runs out, matches get wet, etc. Knowing you can start a fire from nothing if you have to is essential.

But in a true survival situation, nothing beats a lighter for speed and safety. Packed a lighter? Great. Bring two—and keep one in your pocket (warm lighters work better). A canister of waterproof survival matches is a great backup (buy large ones that burn longest—test them at home to find the best).

Redundancy is often the key to survival: Backups should have backups. A magnesium spark rod is a solid backup to matches or a lighter. It never runs out of fuel and can ignite even wet tinder—if you practice. Run the rod against the back (non-blade) side of your knife, experimenting with pressure and stroke length to get a consistent, large shower of sparks.

➤ *Nothing beats matches for lighting a fire.* Credit: istockphoto

There are less conventional ways to light a fire. Want to impress your friends? All you need is steel wool and a nine-volt battery. Pull apart the steel wool to make a bird's nest. Pile tinder and kindling on top. Touch the battery's terminals to the steel wool to set off sparks and embers. Proceed to ignore dropped jaws and popped eyes. This works (though not as easily) with a cell phone battery, too.

But let's say you're caught out in Mother Nature's full wrath without a single incendiary aid. That's when it's time to do as your neolithic forebears did and rely on friction and natural materials. There is no badge of merit, no boon of confidence more desirable than starting a fire without a match. "I can build fire from nothing" is a great way to win anything: cocktail party chatter, free drinks, a date, your life on a frigid night.

Knowing you can use the skills of your Cro-Magnon forebears to bring forth a blaze using nothing more than your hands, sweat, and a couple of sticks feels like the pinnacle of self-reliance. You should hope never to find yourself in a survival situation without a Bic, but if it happens, you won't be the one with hypothermia if you can master the following techniques.

How to Make a Hand Drill

For thousands of years, humans made fire by rubbing two sticks together (aka the hand drill). Here's how to make one.

1. For the spindle and fireboard, find some dry, soft, and non-resinous (no sap) wood—like yucca, cottonwood, poplar, cedar, cypress, or elm—which is easier to create friction with. The spindle stick should be about 16 inches long, ¾-inch thick, and fairly straight. Sharpen the bottom end like a pencil tip, and whittle away any jagged or rough spots on the shaft so you can easily run your hands along it.

2. The fireboard should be about 6 inches long, 1 inch wide, and ¾-inch thick. Carve this rectangular piece so it lies flat on the ground. Cut a V-shaped notch, half as deep as the board, into the edge. Next, carve out a pencil-eraser-size depression at the base of the V, where you will place the spindle tip.

3. Position a leaf, piece of thin bark, or your knife blade (anything as thick as an index card) under the board to catch the coal that will fall out of the board's notch.

4. For the tinder bundle, use what you packed or gathered and shape them into a bird's nest. Place it within arm's reach.

5. Get in a stable kneeling or sitting position, with one foot on the edge of the fireboard to steady it. Put the tip of the spindle in the board's depression, and place your hands at the top. Using significant downward pressure, roll your hands back and forth, up and down the spindle. Go slowly at first to deepen the board's notch. Then go faster (a lot faster), bearing down on the spindle with your body weight as you roll it in your hands. Hot dust will be generated first, then smoke, and as the spindle glows red from the friction,

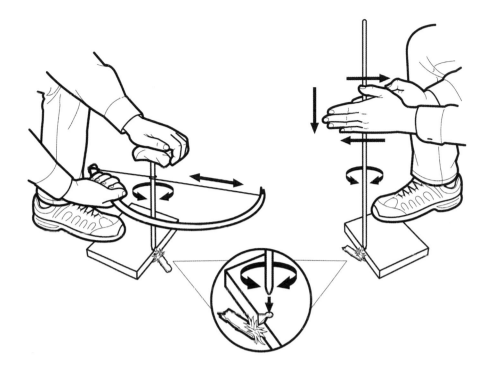

a tiny ember will appear in the notch. If the ember doesn't automatically fall into your catching device, gingerly tap the board.

6. Transfer the ember to the center of the tinder, blow gently until you have flames, then erect small sticks around it, teepee-style.

How to Make a Fire Bow

While the hand drill is the lowest-tech and easiest to build of the rub-two-sticks-together school of fire building, a fire bow gives you a mechanical advantage. Caveat: It has more moving parts and it is harder to perfect technique. But if you can nail it, it can cut your fire-building time in half.

1. **Tie your shoelace** (nylon cordage is even better) to both ends of a curved, strong stick about 2 feet in length. Tie it tight to make a taut-stringed bow.

2. **Carve a point at one end** of another 8-inch straight stick (look for alder, birch, sycamore, or willow) and leave the other end rounded (the drill).

3. In a flat, inch-thick board of soft wood (willow or birch), **whittle a divot** about a half-inch from the edge to accommodate the drill's pointy end, and then cut a V-shaped notch between the hole and edge.

4. **Prep a tinder bundle** using shredded bark, dead leaves, or dry grass, and build a teepee of finger-width sticks.

5. **Step on the board** to hold it in place with the notch positioned over the tinder.

6. **Loop your bow's string once around the drill,** then place the drill in the notch. Lube the rounded end with spit, and hold it in place with a stone in your palm.

7. From down on one knee, **work the bow like a one-handed saw** until an ember forms; when you see a glow or thin wisps of smoke, gently blow on it to coax flames.

8. **Transfer the flaming ember** carefully to your tinder and teepee of sticks.

HACK THIS: ONE MATCH LEFT

Down to your last match? This fast-to-make kindling "bouquet" will light the first time, every time. Here's how you make it.

1. Gather twigs of similar lengths, and no thicker than a pencil.
2. Hold the wider ends in one hand, as you would a bouquet, with the wire-thin tips where the blooms would be.
3. Once your bundle fills one hand, pack the twig ends (the "blooms") with tinder.
4. Invert the bouquet and place it in your fire pit, so it forms a teepee. Wiggle it, if necessary, so it stands.
5. Light from the bottom.

This book is full of survival tips. But you probably didn't know the pages themselves can help in survival. We'd prefer you read it first, but you can put this book to use in an emergency with these nine hacks.

STAY WARM
Stuff your jacket and pants with shredded paper to help retain core warmth. Also: Insulate your feet by cutting out two insole-shaped stacks of pages and putting them in your shoes. Swap in a new "insole" when they get wet.

REALIGN BREAKS
A tube of rolled pages can immobilize anything from a fractured pinky finger or forearm to a tent or hiking pole. Wrap the cylinder tightly around the break, then bind it with tape, cordage, or DIY twine (see "Make Cord," below).

FOSTER FIRE
Paper burns, of course, but you can improve performance in tough conditions. Shred pages finely and buff them up with your hands (like you'd do with natural fibers to make a quick-start tinder). To ignite wet wood, twist dry pages until they're the size of pens and use them as kindling over the shredded tinder. The subsequent heat should be enough to coax damp wood into a campfire.

FEED A FLAME
Roll pages into straw-like tubes and use them to blow oxygen onto coals and get a stubborn fire burning.

SIGNAL HELP
Tear out the brightest pages (contrast with environment is key) and weight them down with sticks and stones to make an SOS sign that's easily visible in an aerial search. Alert ground searchers by leaving bright pages hanging on branches to mark your presence and direction of travel.

MAKE CORD
Tear the pages into long strips, then twist and braid into cord. **Note:** The cord isn't as strong as other natural fibers, so only use it for light-duty applications, like lashing saplings.

DRY BOOTS OR GLOVES
Place strips into your boots like wicks to draw out moisture.

BLOCK BITES AND SCRAPES
Caught out in shorts? Have to bushwhack through nasty vegetation? Fasten rolled pages around your arms and lower legs to protect them against snakebites and thickets.

CATCH A FISH
Twist the brightest pages into small ribbon shapes to make a fish lure that's about as effective as one made from bone or feather. Put the twisted lure directly on the hook (premade or DIY). These have a short lifespan of only a couple of casts, but that's made up for by the ease of manufacturing.

// FEED ME: TIME TO BURN

Fire lit? Congratulations! Wet, cold, lost, hungry: In desperate times, nothing improves your chances of survival more than a roaring blaze. You're probably going to make it—for now. To stay blessedly breathing, you'll need to feed your fire the right way to keep it going. It'll also help if you can determine the anatomy of your fire—where to fuel it, what parts to use for specialized tasks like cooking, and how to get maximum heat for minimum effort. Placing your fuel wood in the right places can create a fire that behaves exactly how you need it to.

What to Place Where

You can just shove any old wood into a fire and it'll burn, right? Wrong. Incorrect placement can singe your dinner into carbon, blow through all your fuel in a few

➤ Credit: istockphoto

short minutes, or even snuff your blaze entirely. Memorize these locations, what to put in them, and when to do it.

1. **Quick Heat** To make your fire roar, add finger- to thumb-thick sticks directly to the top of your blaze. This boosts convection, the movement of super-heated gasses from the bottom to the top, which means the top is the hottest part of the fire. The movement of superheated gasses from the bottom to the top is the campfire's number one source of heat. (It also explains why the top is hottest.) To perk up a flattening fire, or to get a suspended pot boiling quickly, add kindling directly to the top of the blaze.

2. **Cooking Coals** The warmth on your face? That's radiant heat, a much gentler source compared to convection. Add to it by feeding larger fuel onto the sides, then warm your hands or toast your marshmallows without burning them.

3. **Warmth for Hours** Once your fire is well established, add wrist-thick logs around the base. By placing logs in the fire's coolest part, the fuel burns slower, the heat spreads out over time, and the flames last longer without as much attention.

HACK THIS: GAUGE HEAT

When it's time to cook, you'll want to know how hot your coals are. Here's how to tell: Lower your open hand (palm facing up) until it's about 3 inches above the coals and count how long you can hold it. High temp is 1-2 seconds, medium is 4-5, and low is 7-9.

// ALL PUT OUT: BURN OUT, THEN FADE AWAY

You've lit your fire; you've kept it going. You've mastered all the skills you need to keep it going, and you've harnessed it to keep you warm, prepare food, and maybe even signal for help. We're done here, right?

Wrong. If you don't know how to end your fire, you could end up with a blaze strong enough to burn you, your shelter, or the whole damn forest. Don't skip the final step of fire-making—or else. Campfires-gone-amok are the most common source of human-caused wildfires. Make sure yours is out cold.

1. **Let your fire burn all the way down** to ash: no half-burnt sticks or chunky coals.
2. **Douse the ashes** with a few liters of water spread all around it.
3. **Grab a stick and stir,** working the water into the ashes (and sand from your platform if you're using one).
4. Using the back of your hand, **gauge the temperature of the ashes.** If you don't feel any heat 3 inches above, go closer, and closer, until you find them cool to the touch. If you do feel heat, pour on more water and stir.

➤ *Let your fire burn down a little more than this before putitng out.* Credit: istockphoto

5. If you're using an established fire ring, your work is done. If not, when the ashes are cool to the touch, **gather them** and sand from your platform and disperse them widely (at least 200 feet from any water sources).

6. Finally, **scatter the rocks from your fire ring** and collect the tarp or space blanket you laid down. If done properly, the former site of your fire should be undetectable.

HACK THIS: TAMPONS

Tampons have a number of varied uses in survival. Here are a few.

- Dress a wound: Unfold the sterilized cotton and tape it over an open wound or use it to clean a deep cut or stop a bloody nose.
- Make tinder: Pull apart and fluff up the cotton, and dab it with lip balm. Then spark it for the beginnings of a good fire. One tampon has enough cotton to make several tinder bundles.
- Protect matches: Use the plastic wrapper to keep the matches dry.

Why You Should Never Pee on the Fire

I don't remember where I heard that peeing on a fire is a reasonable way to put it out. It certainly seemed reasonable before I tried it. *Here's an on-board supply of waste liquid*, I'd thought. Waste liquid I'd made from beer, because my body is a temple. I remember holding "it" until I figured I'd have plenty for the task, and then, less than a minute into it, thinking, "Dang, my bladder's not big enough." Then, shortly thereafter, uttering a phrase I'm not likely to forget: "Dude, can you help me piss on this fire?" Steam and the acrid smell of warm, pee-scented fumes worked into our clothes and hair and nostrils—and long-term memories. Never try to extinguish a fire with pee; there's not enough beer in the world for the task. *–Casey Lyons*

> Credit: istockphoto

LOST IN AN ALASKAN BLIZZARD

BY JOHN CARLOS MANN,
AS TOLD TO CHASE SCHEINBAUM

// I WAS IN A ROCKY MEADOW, 22 MILES INTO ALASKA'S CHUGACH MOUNTAINS, WHEN THE CAIRNS I WAS FOLLOWING DISAPPEARED.

It was fall, the temperature was close to freezing, and night was coming, casting the rock field in a flat, dusky shade as if all the world was in a shadow. Without a map or compass, I could only trust my gut.

Earlier that day, I had started the 24-mile-long Crow Pass Trail from Eagle River to Girdwood. Most people take two days, starting in Girdwood and losing 3,100 feet of elevation by the time they arrive in Anchorage. But I planned to

do it faster, and in reverse, by myself. My friends were going to an Oktoberfest celebration in Girdwood, and I intended to meet them there.

I'm just a casual Alaskan hiker looking to get in better shape and thought pushing myself on a big day hike would help make that happen. The few friends who might have gone with me weren't available, but I went anyway; I love enjoying the outdoors alone. I'd heard the hike would take about fourteen hours, so I packed a

encounter the trail again. But when I reached the end of the meadow, the creek splintered. I kept pushing. I knew I was lost but I wanted to get to town that night.

As I hiked, I wanted to blame anyone but myself—the meadow really needs cairns—but I knew I was the one who didn't bring a map.

I climbed a slope to a ridge, expecting to see the lights of Girdwood twinkling on the far side. But it was all dark. I was exhausted now, and miserable, but still in good shape. I knew I'd need to sleep out, and that temps might get below freezing. I dug under a huge rock that'd block the breeze, got into my sleeping bag, put the emergency blanket on top like a bivy sack, and put rocks on the corners to keep it in place. My bag was rated to -15°F. It got a little wet, but I was warm.

I woke up before sunrise and climbed on, thinking Girdwood had to be just on the other side of the ridge, but it wasn't. At daybreak, a blizzard blasted the ridge, and I had to trudge through knee-deep snow. I was wearing uninsulated hiking boots, and my feet got cold and started aching badly.

I climbed another ridge, thinking that this time, Girdwood lay on the other side for sure. Reaching the ridgeline felt like a moment of victory. But on the other side there were only more ridges and peaks. I knew I was in trouble and started to beat up on myself for being unprepared. But to turn around would be to admit defeat, so I had to move forward.

Slow Progress

I slid down a steep, snow-covered slope on the far side. I got going pretty fast—faster than I wanted to—and lost a glove. When I stopped, I knew right away that I was on a glacier. I was surrounded by steep ice with nowhere to go but down. I walked carefully for an hour, picking my way around crevasses, until I reached the base. At this point I was really tired and one of my feet was so cold I could feel pain to the bone. I was off the snow by now and took off a shoe—I

headlamp because I figured it would be dark by the time I rolled into Girdwood.

Darkness Spreads

Morning was breaking when my buddy dropped me off at the trailhead. Just in case, I'd packed my down sleeping bag, an insulated jacket and pants, a raincoat, and an emergency blanket. I didn't bring a tent, though, or a map and compass—it's a popular route, and I thought the trail would be easy enough to follow.

Darkness spread as soon as I lost the trail, which had been following a stream. I deduced that if I just continued along the stream, I'd soon

> Credit: istockphoto

HACK THIS: SELF-DIAGNOSE HYPOTHERMIA

Here's the thing about hypothermia: If you have it, your brain will be too fuzzed up to realize it. Here's the other thing: If you don't actively treat hypothermia, it only gets worse. When hiking with a buddy, check in with your partner and diagnose hypothermia's telltale "umbles": stumbles, mumbles, fumbles, and grumbles. Not so easy by yourself. I once asked Jennifer Dow, medical director for the National Park Service's Alaska region, for her best tips on how to do it solo.

1. Think of hypothermia as a continuum. Cold is the first step. If you feel chilled and/or your clothing is wet, stop, adjust your layers, or change into dry clothes, and eat sugar and protein for fuel.

2. Pay attention to your fine motor skills. Dropping your gloves? Can't tie your shoes? Having a hard time zipping your jacket? Don't brush off these warning signs. The early signs of hypothermia are a lot like early signs of being drunk.

3. Take shivering seriously. This may be your last chance to head off more severe hypothermia. Shivering is the body's frantic effort to heat itself, and it burns a ton of fuel attempting to do so. Consider this your final warning.

4. Above all, know when hypothermia could affect you. Hypothermia is more common at milder temperatures than subfreezing ones, because people heading out into freezing conditions are generally prepared for them, Dow says.

don't know why—and walked like that for thirty minutes. Maybe it was adrenaline, maybe numbness, but the pain faded.

I came across a huge creek that I figured drained into Turnagain Arm, and could at least lead me to the Seward Highway. I followed it through steep terrain, dense alders, and downed trees. My feet got really wet crossing several small streams, and I ate the last of my food. I bushwhacked along the creek, climbing to avoid the densest vegetation and descending to make sure I stayed by the creek. Progress was really slow, and I began to feel more and more defeated. I thought about throwing myself onto the boulders in the creek. They would rip me apart. It would be over so fast.

Finally, I reached a moose trail. There were some flat sections, and I put in several miles very fast. I pushed into falling darkness until I was unable to see, turned on my headlamp, and kept going to get as much distance as I could. When I came to a fallen tree, at about 3 a.m., I decided I needed rest. Everything I had was wet, but I crawled into my down sleeping bag again, wrapped it in the emergency blanket, and put rocks on the corners, which made the thin material start to tear in the wind. For several hours I shivered badly, sometimes going numb. I hardly slept. I just lay there in a trance.

Sunday proved to be the most challenging day because I was utterly spent. The vegetation got thick again, and my legs were so tired I could barely lift them. I was delirious. I sang songs and recited poems. One was the epigraph of Jack London's *The Call of the Wild*:

> *Old longings nomadic leap,*
> *Chafing at custom's chain;*
> *Again from its brumal sleep*
> *Wakens the ferine strain.*

By the afternoon, I still hadn't found a road. I realized that I could die out there. Around 3 p.m., I felt like I needed sleep. I removed my wet shoes and socks and pulled out my soaked-through sleeping bag. I got in and ten minutes later, I was shivering crazily. I could feel my arms and legs going numb. The veins in my hands were bright blue.

Guided by Moonlight

I was thinking of my mom, of her hearing the news that her son died. I'm an only child. I thought about my friends, too, but mostly my family. I knew if I was to stay that night, I was not going to wake up. I said to myself, *I'm not going to go out without a fight*. I put my shoes and socks back on and wrapped my hands and feet in the shreds of the emergency blanket. I could barely feel my knees or ankles. I was staggering like a drunk.

My headlamp was dead now, but just then I saw something magnificent: a little piece of orange tape hanging on a branch. It had been two days since I saw anything man-made. A little while later, I saw a cut I knew was made by a chain saw. Sure enough, minutes later, I found another piece of orange tape and then a trail. It wasn't well maintained, but it led to a tiny parking lot for ATVs.

I followed this trail in complete darkness, guided only by dim moonlight reflecting on pools of water in the ATV trail. I was crying out loud for help. Eventually, I saw another magnificent sight: lights in the windows of homes. I was in a lot of pain. I cried for help but no one came outside. In my delirium, I decided not to bother these people because I knew the highway was close by.

I tried to hitchhike, but no one would stop at 10:30 p.m. I looked like a miserable, beat-up homeless guy. Probably a hundred cars went by and none stopped. Finally, I made it to a rustic motel, the Birdridge Motel & RV Park. I saw people inside the living room. I said, "Please help! I'm not a bandit." After five minutes of this, a man opened the door. He was the kindest person. He was with his wife and three kids—one was a newborn baby.

He poured me chicken broth and hot tea, and lit the wood stove. It only took twenty minutes for me to start feeling better. It was the best cup of chicken broth I ever tasted.

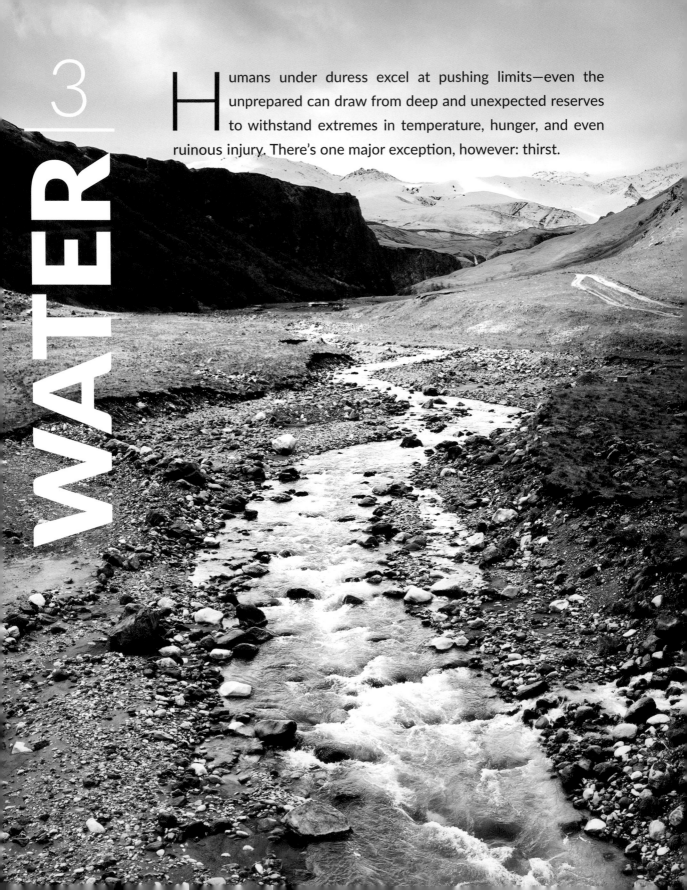

WATER

3

umans under duress excel at pushing limits—even the unprepared can draw from deep and unexpected reserves to withstand extremes in temperature, hunger, and even ruinous injury. There's one major exception, however: thirst.

Without a drink, a hiker can die in as little as a day. In the best of situations, even Bear Grylls won't last beyond three.

Still, most hikers don't pack enough water or research sources before they head out. I've spotted sips for parched newbies on the way to the bottom of the Grand Canyon; one time, when I arrived I found two half-delirious college kids in jeans and black t-shirts taking a desperate jump into the swift, icy Colorado just to take a drink. I didn't have the heart to tell them their pockets wouldn't hold enough for the trip back up to the rim (they didn't bring a tent).

But even experienced adventurers get caught high and dry. You'd be hard pressed to find as experienced a desert rambler as *BACKPACKER* Southwest field editor Annette McGivney, but even she can relate:

"Eight years ago, a friend and I were hiking Jump Up Canyon in Kanab Creek Wilderness on the Grand Canyon's North Rim, with big plans to hike across the Esplanade and around Fishtail Point to Thunder River (40 miles, one way). The Esplanade is a long slickrock bench about 2,000 feet below the rim. It's great for views, but lacks reliable springs. It was May, though, and we figured the potholes scattered across the Esplanade would contain water from snowmelt and recent rain.

"Five miles into the Esplanade traverse, we found about three liters in a few shallow potholes and cut a dry camp. By midafternoon the next day, in temperatures that climbed into the 90s, we'd gotten dangerously low on water. Then we came across a series of large, shallow pools, each about 4 inches deep and the diameter of a VW Beetle. After setting up camp, we drank a few liters, boiled water for pasta, and rejoiced that our instincts had been rewarded. We felt rich with water.

"That's when we made a crucial error. Before going to sleep, we failed to refill our bottles. When we awoke the next morning, all the water was gone. Overnight, it had evaporated completely, leaving only mud. We decided to turn around and backtrack 15 miles on exposed slickrock that we knew contained no water. We each had about half a liter. It was a hot, hard, and agonizing day, because we knew there was no margin for error. Now, in the desert, I never pass up a chance for a refill."

Our societies follow water to stay alive (with some exceptions—looking at you, Las Vegas). In the wild, you're best off doing the same. Bring all the water you need, or plan on finding and securing reliable water sources from ponds, rivers, or pools. Even if it's befouled or you have no way of treating it, drink it. Dehydration will kill you faster than infection. Factory worker Reshma Begum survived for sixteen days pinned by rubble after a factory collapse in Bangladesh. Injured and without access to food, experts say the key to her survival was water: Even small dribbles kept her hydrated enough to await rescue and get pulled out on the seventeenth day. The lesson? Drink up.

➤ *Drink up.* Credit: istockphoto

// WET WORKS: SIP FOR SUCCESS

How much water does a body need? That depends on conditions, exertion, even the individual needs of different bodies. A very wide ballpark is about a half cup to a cup for every thirty minutes of a hike, which means eight hours of hiking requires a bare minimum 2 liters of water (and likely very much more). That's 4.4 pounds of water. You can begin to see why many hikers don't bring enough, and why savvy hikers plan to procure water while on a hike.

By all means obey your thirst. But keep in mind thirst isn't necessarily the best indicator for staying hydrated. Pay attention to the following factors, and you can keep dehydration at bay well before it catches up to you.

Drink on a Schedule

Don't just wait until you're thirsty to drink. Feeling thirsty is usually the first sign you're on the road to dehydration, and liquid can take as long as two hours to actually circulate into your system. Start drinking water before your activity starts and sip a little every fifteen minutes on hot days.

Eat Carbs and Don't Forget Electrolytes

The body converts carbs into glycogen, which binds to water and helps you retain more water. Incorporate carbs into hourly snacks. Supplementing water with a sports drink that contains electrolytes helps prevent hyponatremia (low blood sodium; see below).

Go for the Big Gulp and Drink at the Source

There's some evidence that taking a few healthy pulls off your water bottle is better than bird sips. The increased pressure on your stomach from a higher volume of water speeds absorption. But don't go overboard: A belly full of water slows it

HACK THIS: WARM WATER

The body absorbs cold water faster than warm water, and cold water encourages regular drinking because it's freaking delicious. On hot days, do as the pros do and bring one frozen water bottle that melts during the day.

down. In dry conditions, where chances to refill are few and far between, camp near a water source and chug at least a liter before leaving. This enables you to start hydrated and carry less (if safe).

Know the Signs and Watch Your Pee Color

Headache, dry mouth, and confusion are all symptoms of dehydration. If your urine is apple juice–colored, you're dehydrated. If it's as clear as water, you might be overhydrated and at risk for hyponatremia. Drink enough water that your pee remains a pale yellow.

// DRINKING PROBLEM: FINDING EMERGENCY WATER

So you did everything right—or maybe you didn't—but you got lost and ran out of water. Most wild areas are crisscrossed by streams and dotted with ponds: If you find them, drink from them. Waterborne illness takes days or even weeks to set in, so stay hydrated, even if that means some extra toilet time when you arrive home.

But even some mountainous areas can be surprisingly dry, especially in late summer. Don't panic: In most cases, finding water is more effective than conjuring it. In almost any ecosystem, the same landscape features yield water. Here are some rough guides.

> *Search for potholes for a water source.* Credit: istockphoto

Scout High and Early, and Follow Shade

If your supply runs out, climb to a hilltop and look for signs of water. Especially in the early morning, when the water table is at its highest, reflections of pools are easier to spot, and birds and insects often swarm wet areas. Look in shady areas at the bases of cliffs, for pockets and depressions in rock, and in the undercut banks of dry streambeds.

Track Tracks—Look for the Birds and the Bees

Look for big and small: Deer, bighorn sheep, mountain goats, and big animals usually converge near water sources, but so do raccoons and possums. Follow birds and insects; tree hollows sometimes hold water weeks after rainfall. Honeybees and songbirds are especially good indicators of nearby water.

HACK THIS: SURVIVAL STRAW

In desperate situations you might find water, only to discover a nasty surprise when it's impossible to collect that water into a tall bottle or cup from a shallow puddle. No worries: Sip with a straw or hydration tube (many water bottles have an internal tube). If you don't have either, look for hollow reeds near drainages. Pay attention: Reeds mean water could be near. Worst-case scenario: Soak up water with a bandanna or shirt and wring it into a container.

Green Is Good

Vegetation that indicates water includes cottonwood trees (roots can go 40 to 60 feet down, so you might not be able to dig far enough), willows, cattails, velvet ash, sycamore, mesquite, and Bermuda grass.

Search for Potholes

Potholes (also called tinajas) can be found in sandstone or rock in shady areas, especially at the bottoms of cliffs and ravines. The water is often standing and scummy, but water is water.

Well: Dig It

Dry riverbeds and sandy washes are often more than they seem: Sometimes digging into them will yield a drink. Outer bends and depressions are best, because they're the last places water would have evaporated from.

First, look for washes that show signs of vegetation or animal life nearby. The hole should be 1 to 2 feet deep, and preferably on the outer bend of the wash. It could take up to an hour for water to seep into the hole if it's down there.

This method also can be used in coastal regions where no fresh water is in the vicinity: Dig the hole on the inland side of sand dunes. Several wells will improve your odds, and if all you get is mud, wring it out in a bandanna to extract the moisture.

// DEHYDRATION: AN ANATOMY

As mentioned above, if you're getting thirsty, you're getting closer and closer to "too late." But you're not reading this book because everything goes according to plan. If you know what happens to the body when under dehydration duress, you'll know just how desperate you are—and how to react accordingly.

Mouth

Dry mouth begins in as few as 15 minutes. As your body loses its ability to make saliva, your tongue will swell, your lips will crack, and your gums will bleed. If you're

➤ *Know the signs of dehydration.* Credit: istockphoto

in unrelenting heat for several hours without a sip of water, sores inside your parched throat will make swallowing very painful.

Excretory System

The body sheds electrolytes via sweat and urine. You know dehydration has taken hold when you notice a decrease in urine (what little you have will be dark yellow or amber with a strong odor), dried-up tear ducts, and a sandpaper-like throat. If you stop sweating altogether, that's bad news: Your body has completely run dry.

Heart

Without ample hydration, blood thickens, forcing the heart to work harder to circulate it. The added stress causes your heart rate to spike from its resting rate of 60 to 100 beats per minute to 100 to 120. Over several hours, a quickened pulse can impair the heart's overall efficiency and lead to severe dizziness, fainting, and an increased chance of cardiac arrest.

Cells

The body tries to leach water from cell membranes. Consequently, each cell's outer membrane hardens in an attempt to barricade the H_2O inside. As a result, hormones like dopamine can't flow in, and waste products that damage the cell can't flow out. This can lead to muscular fatigue, blood pressure imbalances, and eventually stomach ulcers.

Brain

Your gray matter is 73 percent water, and thus one of the organs most susceptible to a lack of moisture. Just ninety minutes of profuse sweating can shrink the brain as much as an entire year's worth of aging. Robbed of the essential minerals it needs to function, your brain may take up to twice as long to process information. Cognition recovers quickly after you hydrate.

HACK THIS: MURKY WATER

Dirty water clogs filters, hampers UV purification, and makes chemical treatments less effective. Here's how to find a better water source, or to clean what you have.

1. **Scout for a clearer source.** Good bets include pond inlets, rocky streams, and headwaters—such as where water springs from the ground or runs from a snowfield. Turbid water is more likely after floods, forest fires, and spring runoff, or downstream of canyons, deserts, and moraines.

2. **Strain the silt.** In a hurry? You can cover your bottle's mouth with a coffee filter, bandanna, sock, or shirt, fill it with water, then pump or treat the bottled water.

3. **Let it settle.** If you can wait a while, let the water sit in your cookpot overnight (cover it to keep critters out), then carefully ladle the top, clear layer into another container and pump it or use a UV device or chemical treatment.

4. **Set up a capillary filter.** If you're short on water but long on time, dip one tip of a wet bandanna into an elevated bottle containing the murky water, then put the other tip into an empty bottle situated below the first one. Clean water will be wicked along the fabric and drip into your container. Caveat: It takes about an hour to filter one cup, and you still have to treat it.

5. **Boil for one minute.** Though boiling burns time and fuel, it packs a double punch: The heat kills pathogens, and the boiling action settles sediment. Extract the clear layer when done.

// WATER, WATER NOWHERE: CONJURING IT

But what if you're stranded in a parched desert, far from identifiable water sources? This is far from ideal: Finding water is almost always easier and yields more than procuring it out of a bone-dry environment. But you have options. Here are three techniques for conjuring H_2O out of thin air. Some are techniques old as the dirt you'll be divining for water; some require trash from space-age materials. With lots of practice, they all work.

➤ *Collect water from the morning dew that gathers on plants.* Credit: istockphoto

Dew Harvesting

Even the driest desert gets a little wet. When air cools at night, atmospheric moisture condenses and forms water droplets on exposed surfaces. Simply use a cloth or T-shirt to sop up the moisture and wring it out into your mouth. Ignore advice about tying T-shirts to your feet and tripping through the weeds: It's easier to wipe your cloth-covered hand on dense, broad-leafed vegetation and grass. You might also sop up bugs, dirt, bird poop, and plant toxins; if possible, treat before drinking.

Sopping up dew yields the most water for the least effort. Using a Buff head covering or a scarf, you can squeeze a cup of water from a shaded, saturated bush in a few minutes. Expect good results on cool nights in humid, wind-free climates, in areas with moist soil, and along damp depressions and stream channels.

Tip: In arid environments (high altitude, deserts), work fast when dew is present (usually from the coldest portion of night until sunrise). Wind, dry air, and sudden temperature increases can evaporate it quickly.

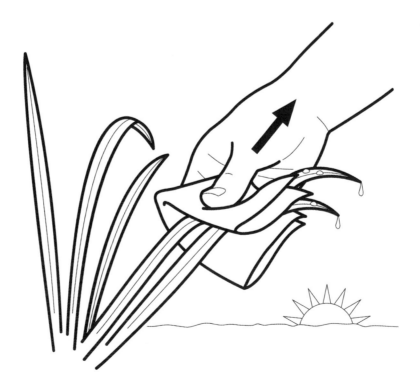

Solar Still

Have a puddle of putrid water—or nothing to drink besides your own pee? If you have a piece of plastic and a container, then you can purify water in a pinch with a solar still, which extracts moisture from questionable sources but leaves most unsavory elements (bacteria, toxins, dirt) behind.

Best bet: Find an existing hole in a sunny area. Next best: Dig a 2-by-2-foot hole with a flat bottom, or several smaller holes if the ground is hard. Add green vegetation, non-potable water or urine to your hole, then place a cup or container in the center, taking care to not get any of your questionable water in the cup itself. Spread a watertight material (rainfly, plastic, synthetic jacket) over the hole, pull taut, and seal the edges using rocks and soil. Use a stone to weight the sheet above the cup so the water drips into it.

This technique is best for wringing pure water from a plentiful but questionable supply (salty, muddy, choked with dead possums). It takes a long time: I once left a still out under four hours of partial sunlight, and the still yielded about a quarter-cup of water from moist earth, a couple handfuls of succulent green leaves, and a sprinkle of urine. The evaporated water was drinkable, but be forewarned: Some of the taste (if not the toxins) from your source will come through.

Tip: Save sweat by digging at night in soft soil.

Transpiration Bag

Place a smooth rock in the bottom corner of a plastic bag (the clearer and larger, the better). Pull the bag over a leafy branch. Tie it so air can't escape. Wait a few hours, until water collects in the bag's weighted corner. Untie the bag and pour the water into a container to drink. Works best with succulents and bright green, broad-leafed plants.

This set-it-and-forget-it method can supplement your survival needs, but don't count on it as your sole supply–unless you have two dozen plastic bags. This technique produced only a few teaspoons of water in four hours.

Tip: Because heat will cause the plant's pores to close, you'll get the best results in the morning and evening.

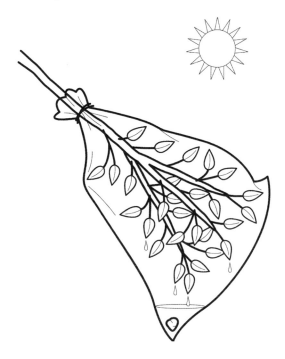

If you're caught out in the wild and low on water, don't run dry. You can help avoid death-by-desiccation by conserving water in the first place.

1. Chill in wind-free shade and avoid exertion during the hottest time of day, from 11 a.m. to 4:30 p.m.
2. Eat less, especially proteins. Metabolizing high-protein foods speeds dehydration. Exception: fruits and veggies, which contain water.
3. Inhale and exhale through your nose. Mouth-breathing is more than embarrassing—it costs you water.
4. Keep your shirt on. Adults lose an average of 14 ounces of water per day through the skin. Keep it cool and covered to slow the process. Soak your clothes to prevent sweating.
5. Ration water wisely, but don't deprive yourself; sip at regular intervals.

HACK THIS: SNOW AND ICE

Dehydration can strike in any condition—even in cold and water. But eating snow or ice directly over a prolonged period can compound your chances for hypothermia. Fill a bottle or container with ice or snow and tuck it in between your layers so body heat melts it.

// IN HOT WATER: EMERGENCY PURIFICATION

It bears repeating: If faced with the choice of dehydration or drinking mucky water, drink the goddamn water. That said, if your timeline for rescue is uncertain or you've just lost the ability to purify water but remain safe, some clever DIY methods can keep microbial invaders from wrecking your gut. Gastrointestinal distress is much more serious than a ruined pair of Prana pants; once symptoms set in, the resulting diarrhea and dehydration will drop you like a lesser family member on the Oregon Trail. Here's how to keep your questionable quaffage clean.

Boil Water in Anything

You're lost and dehydrated when you stumble across salvation: a muck-rimmed pool. The problem? You need to zap the water free of microbial gremlins before you can drink it or use it to clean wounds. But all you have is an empty water bottle—or worse, nothing at all. Here's your solution.

BOIL WATER IN A BOTTLE
Boil water in a plastic bottle using just a stick, a shoelace, and a hot fire.

➤ Credit: istockphoto

1. **Prep the Fire:** Let the flames settle into red-hot coals. (You can heat a bottle over flames, but it'll deform—often making it single-use.) Using a stick as a poker, create a 3-inch, bowl-like depression in the coals, wide enough to surround your bottle without risk of contact, and deep enough to evenly distribute heat around the bottle.

2. **Prep the Bottle:** (a) Fill your vessel with water (if the water is gunky, strain it through a T-shirt or bandanna first) and remove the cap (otherwise, built-up pressure could cause a scalding overflow when you unscrew it). (b) Loop a shoelace under the lip of the bottle and tie it tight with an overhand knot. (c) Fasten the other end of the shoelace to a 2- to 3-foot-long stick. (d) Carefully lower the bottle into the depression, keeping it suspended just a few inches from the coals. (Tip: Use a Y-shaped stick to make a natural tripod.)

You should be able to boil two cups of water in ten to fifteen minutes. The bottle may deform slightly, but it shouldn't blacken. Water boiled this way will have a faint plastic aftertaste, and there is considerable debate about the long-term danger posed by leached chemicals.

BOILING WITH HOT ROCKS

Can't find a plastic (or glass or metal) bottle? You can still boil in almost any vessel that holds water—even a plastic bag or your hat—using this technique.

1. **Prep the Container:** You can use almost anything that holds liquid. In a pinch, even a plastic bag or tarp will do. Dig a shallow hole (4 inches deep) near your fire and line the depression with the bag or tarp. Weight the plastic (edges and center) with small stones. Put a layer of cool rocks in the bottom of the bag—this will insulate it and keep the bottom from melting. You can also prop up a plastic bag with sticks, which is less energy-intensive, but riskier. Fill the plastic bag halfway with water.

2. **Prep the Stones:** Gather a handful of egg-size stones (basalt and quartzite work best) and put them in the fire. (*Safety note:* Don't collect stones from riverbeds, as any rocks with moisture or sand in them can explode when heated.) Leave them in the coals for ten minutes (they'll start to turn pale), then gather them using a split, thumb-width stick as tongs. Drop the hot rocks into the water-filled vessel one at a time, placing them carefully on top of the cool, submerged stones. You'll see bubbles form on the side of

HACK THIS: MAKE A BOWL OUT OF BARK

Got trees? You can make a drinking and boiling vessel from bark. (1) Peel off a sheet of the outer bark of a birch or willow (a Leave No Trace no-no, but this is survival) and cut it into a 10-inch-diameter circle. Soak the bark to make it more pliable. (2) Make a cup out of the bark by folding it in half twice. Once it's quartered, spread the top so it resembles a pointy water cooler cup. (3) Pin it shut by slitting open a small branch at the end and using it like a clothespin. This origami technique will also work with a waterproof map. An alternate option, if you have time, is making a burn bowl: Burn out the inside of a log until you've got a pot-size bowl you can rock-boil in and carry with you.

the bag as the water begins to boil. Let it boil for at least five minutes, and drink when cool. Slowly but surely, you can boil 2 cups of water in about ten minutes. The result will be ashy—maybe not the best-tasting water, but free from stomach-wrecking toxins.

Improvised Filters

Boiling is usually best, but there are other improvised methods that can improve water quality. Interestingly, most function on the same principles as commercially available filters. With a little ingenuity, you can recreate these mechanisms in the backcountry.

CHARCOAL FILTER

Activated charcoal powers many popular filters: The porous surface captures some (but not all) contaminants. To build a charcoal filter, cut the bottom off a disposable plastic bottle (or use a birch-bark bowl as a funnel). Fasten cloth from a T-shirt to the opening and turn upside down. Fill the container with a layer of crushed charcoal

> *If you've got charcoal, you're one step closer to a workable filter.* Credit: istockphoto

from your campfire, followed by a layer of sand, a layer of gravel, and then a layer of vegetation (iodine-rich sphagnum moss is best—it's the carpet-like moss you find in bogs and on old logs in conifer forests). Position it over a drinking vessel, and pour contaminated water into your improvised filter. Each successive layer will remove contaminants from the water before it reaches your drinking vessel. It isn't guaranteed to remove all pathogens, but it's better than drinking raw water from a pothole.

SUN FILTER

Popular new filtration wands like SteriPENs use blasts of UV light to kill a wide range of microbes (including viruses, which some filters miss). You have access to UV rays, too: Clear water less than four inches deep can be cleaned with prolonged exposure to sunlight. Exposed water is best, but you can leave plastic or glass exposed to full sun rays for a few hours to kill microbes. Partially cloudy days require more hours, and the method gets less reliable.

These much-maligned Christmas presents turn out to be handy survival hacks. Here are seven reasons to pack an extra pair.

MAKE WATER
Fill a sock with mud or wet clay, then wring out every drop of moisture.

WARM YOUR HANDS
This could prevent frostbite and restore dexterity. It's very hard to make a lifesaving fire with numb fingers.

JURY-RIG CRAMPONS
To create traction on slick ice, pull a wool (it's stickier than nylon and polyester materials) sock over the toe of your boot. The fibers adhere to ice.

MAKE A DEADMAN ANCHOR
Fill a sock with sand or snow, then tie to a guyline and bury it to create a shelter anchor.

FASHION A HUNTING WEAPON
Starving? Stuff a sock with stones to create a sort of nunchuck for clubbing small game.

CARRY A SNAKE
If you catch one, tie it off inside a sock to keep it alive until you need to eat it. Come to think of it, this works with mice and birds, too—anything that fits inside that you can get your hands on.

FILTER WATER
It will remove sediment, but not all bacteria and other microorganisms. Fill your sock with sand, charcoal, and grass to grab the bigger particles, and pour water through. It may taste a little ripe, but it's safer than drinking it straight.

DRINK YOUR PEE?

Don't do it. Take it from me: Piss tastes like piss. It's full of salt and much less refreshing than seawater, which you shouldn't drink either. Assuming you can get it down, you'll survive a serving. But if all you're sipping is urine, the concentrated toxins will overwhelm your kidneys within days and kill you. Determined to make use of your own urine? Collect pee in a bottle and purify using a solar still. Or pee on your clothing to reduce sweat loss during the hottest parts of the day.

// HEATSTROKE: AN ANATOMY

Only 6 degrees of body temperature separate feeling good and feeling like you're melting. Heat is responsible for more deaths than all other outdoor hazards combined: Dozens of people die every year of heat-related illnesses in state and national parks alone. Learn how your body responds to high temps and what you can do to cool down.

98.6°F (normal)

Heating up: As heat builds in the core, the body moves it to the skin. Your primary cooling mechanism—sweating—begins. (The body loses between 0.8 and 1.4 liters per hour, depending on conditions and fitness.) Excess ambient heat amplifies internal temperature, so avoid exercise during the hottest part of the day (12 to 4 p.m.). Jumping into hot conditions can be dangerous if you're not acclimated: Your body doesn't have time to adjust its sweat output or regulate core temperature.

Cooling down: Wear loose, light-colored clothing, which reflects heat and allows it to escape. Use a water reservoir to encourage regular sipping and optimal hydration. Wear a full-brimmed hat and water-resistant sunscreen (SPF 15 or higher). Seek shade, where heat index values decrease as much as 15°F. Heat-acclimate in advance of hot weather trips by exercising in conditions like those you'll encounter for sixty minutes a day for two weeks.

98.6-104°F (heat exhaustion)

Heating up: Sweating intensifies (up to three liters per hour). Weakness, confusion, and dizziness increase with rising body temperature. Heat syncope (heat-related fainting) occurs when increased blood flow to the skin causes a critical lack of blood flow to the brain. Nausea and loss of appetite result from electrolyte imbalances (the body purges essential salts while sweating). Heartbeat won't slow below 100 beats per minute.

Cooling down: Drink enough water (one liter per hour) to replace most of what you've lost to sweat and urination, but don't exceed twelve liters in a day, or you'll risk water intoxication (hyponatremia). Pour water on clothes (rather than stripping) to increase evaporative cooling. Replenish electrolytes with sports drinks or salty snacks. Rest, preferably in the shade, until your pulse returns to below 100 beats per minute.

104°F-plus (heatstroke)

Heating up: Skin is flushed, but sweating stops. Pupils narrow. The too-hot brain malfunctions, causing light-headedness and disorientation. Seizures can occur due to lack of blood flow. Electrolyte imbalances cause vomiting. Breathing becomes irregular (deep breaths and shallow ones).

Cooling down: Call for rescue! Heatstroke (aka sunstroke) is a life-threatening condition and death or permanent damage can occur if the victim is not cooled down within thirty minutes. Look for a river or a spring: Complete immersion in cold water is the most rapid method of lowering body temperature. No luck? Put water, wet clothes, or snow bags on areas where blood vessels are closest to the surface: neck, armpits, back, and groin. Lie the victim on his or her back with their feet higher than their head to prevent shock.

LOST IN THE DESERT

BY ED ROSENTHAL AS TOLD TO JOSHUA PRESTIN

// I COULD SEE THE LIGHTS OF CIVILIZATION 10 MILES IN THE DISTANCE, PROMISING SALVATION.

But I was too thirsty and tired and sunbaked to answer the call. I could barely move. No one knew where I was. The lights glimmered like a cruel mirage.

I had set out solo four days earlier, on Friday morning, for a celebratory day hike up to 4,900-foot Warren View, a peak in Joshua Tree National Park—my long-standing ritual after closing big real estate deals. I knew it was only an hour and a half—less than 3 miles—to the top, so I didn't

bother to top off the half-quart of water left in my hydration pack or bring maps. I grabbed my day pack, which had most of the 10 Essentials, but left my jacket and layers in the car. I basked in the cleansing 90°F September sun as I climbed.

To the southwest, 10,834-foot San Jacinto Peak dominated the horizon as I ate lunch at Warren View, and I scanned the contours of the San Andreas Fault, absorbing the wide desert vistas and the feeling of being on top of my game. But then, when I turned to head back, something wasn't right.

Lost in the Desert

I couldn't make out the little-used, rocky trail. I had passed a sign on my way up that read West Trail, but when I descended I missed it. I couldn't clearly recall the landmarks I'd used to navigate back before. Everywhere I looked appeared unfamiliar. I scurried the quarter-mile between Warren View and Warren Peak and finally spotted what looked like a terraced ravine that ran toward where I thought the trailhead was. I went for it, thinking it would intersect the main trail.

I wove downhill between cacti, leaning hard on my hiking pole on the 40-degree slope. Three times I had to jump down rock faces, each time realizing the climb back up would be impossible. After the last 15-foot downclimb I admitted to myself that I was following a dry creek bed—no trail in sight—and I had no clue where I was going.

But the answer had to be downhill. I stumbled along for another half-mile, and then suddenly, miraculously, stepped out onto a real trail. *It's going downhill*, I thought. *Out of the mountains!* I followed it for three hours, charging ahead in pursuit of fuchsia and yellow prickly pear blooms that I mistook for hikers' shirts. Each time I turned a corner my hope was swallowed by the vastness of the folded terrain. I could see the desert changing form ahead, flattening out into a sea of dust and scrub brush shimmering with waves of heat. I knew I'd transitioned from the Mojave into the Colorado Desert—a hotter, more hostile land.

I turned around and worked my way off-trail to a sandy depression where, six hours after I started my day hike, I hunkered down for the night. I could see airplane lights blinking rhythmically overhead and I signaled to them by flashing my headlamp against my emergency blanket, but it was no use. No one even knew I was lost;

"I PREPARED MY MIND FOR THE POSSIBILITY THAT I MIGHT DIE SOON."

I wasn't supposed to check in with my wife until Monday (I was on a day hike, but planned to be away longer), and that was two days away.

Morning Light, No Relief

Dawn prodded me awake, and I tried eating some dates I had in my pack. I chewed and chewed, but without saliva, they stuck to the roof of my mouth like peanut butter, making me gag. I was already dehydrated, and I'd finished my water the afternoon before. I tried sucking on pebbles to create saliva, but nothing happened. I tried to drink my urine, but spat it out.

I retraced my route back down to the trail, and stood at the mouth of a red-hued canyon, trying to discern where to go. Thirty or more trails spun into the desert. I picked a path that looked like it was made by humans. I knew I could backtrack and try another trail if this one led nowhere, but wasn't sure I could stand much trial-and-error—I was thirsty, tired, and depleted. (I later learned I'd hiked 18 miles.)

The sun beat down, drying out my nose and mouth until they felt like rubber. Exhausted and panting, I stumbled to a lone evergreen set on a tall hill and crawled under its branches for relief and shade. I fell asleep immediately. Every hour or so the sun shifted enough to burn my legs. I crawled back into the safety of the shade and collapsed again.

When the heat of the day relented, I knew I had to find water. I'd been without it for more than 24 hours, and knew I wouldn't make it

▶ Credit: Michael Darter

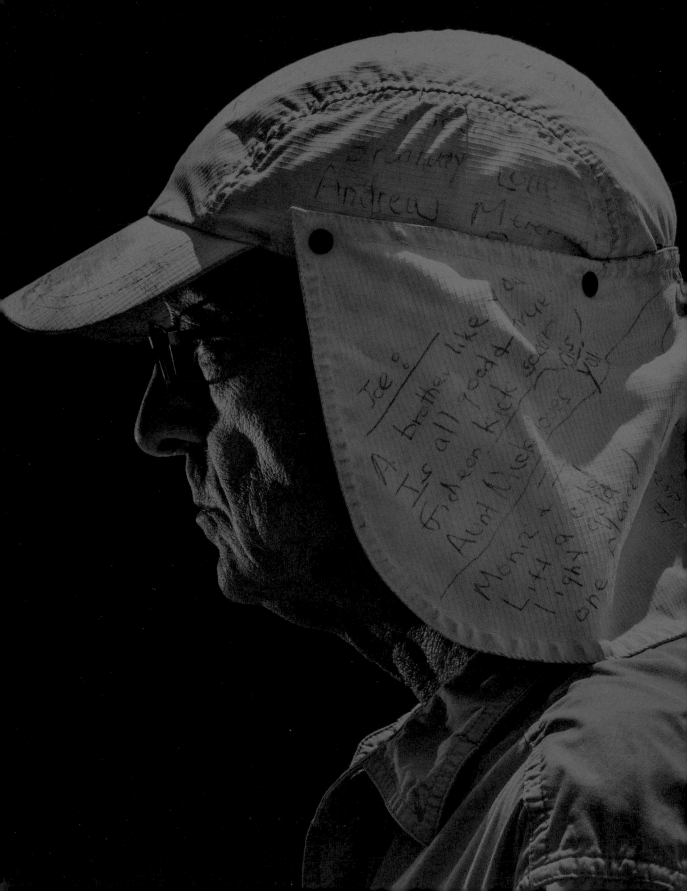

much longer. I thought I could squeeze water from a yucca plant, and I pried at its pistachio-colored flesh with my knife to no avail. I couldn't get it to produce a single drop.

As the sun set, I found myself hundreds of feet higher than the lone pine tree, and the air cooled fast. I tried to start a fire with my survival matches, but my hands were shaky, and I couldn't find enough fuel. No combination of flame and tinder could keep my pile of twigs lit, so I pulled a roll of toilet paper (I didn't think to try it as tinder) from my pack and wrapped it around my arms and legs to substitute for the warm layers I'd left at the trailhead.

When the first shiver hit me I felt truly afraid. I didn't think I was strong enough to fight hypothermia. I'd survived a heart attack several years before, and vowed to never get worked up again. It took all I had to calm myself through the night, and I spent hours watching Orion and Vega spin overhead.

Sleep, Burn, Crawl

The next morning brought me two goals: Stay in the shade, and find a warmer place to sleep. I'd given up on self-rescue. I rose, weakly, and moved downhill. I attacked the yucca fronds again to no avail. (I'd later learn that yucca don't produce drinkable water; neither do most cacti.) Within a mile I was too hot to carry on—each time I sat down I struggled to get up. I crawled under a rock and repeated my dance with the midday sun. Sleep, burn, crawl. Sleep, burn, crawl. I awoke once to notice a small canyon 50 yards away. I stumbled into it and collapsed in the shade, only moving when the sliver of sun at the bottom touched my skin.

Each time I moved I felt my strength leave me. I thought about my wife and twenty-year-old daughter at home and how I missed them,

and I scribbled messages to each of them on my hat in case someone found my body. I said the Shema Yisrael—a Jewish end-of-life prayer—and prepared my mind for the possibility that I might die soon.

When the stars faded above my canyon, I was too weak to move far. All I could do was crawl after the shade as it eluded me along the vertical wall. A fly buzzed around my head. It was the only living thing I saw, but it brought me comfort to know I wasn't alone.

Tuesday I awoke to the sight of Orion in the morning sky, and I felt strong enough to try signaling rescuers again. I limped 40 yards to a clump of tall, dead grass against the canyon wall and lit it. I struggled back to the shade and watched it emit smoke for fifteen minutes before the fuel was gone. I sat and waited for what felt like ages, but nothing happened. I was still all alone. I crawled back to my shade and fitfully slept. I was out of fire-starters. I was out of options. I was spent.

Power of Prayer

When I awoke on Wednesday I couldn't move at all. I lay on a rock and stared at the sky, praying for rain. Miraculously, it came.

Intermittent showers doused me with cool drops and soothed my parched mouth. I dozed between showers, thankful for a respite from the heat and sun. I didn't have the energy to try to gather rain. I didn't even try. All I could do was lay still, mouth open, at nature's mercy.

The next morning I didn't wake up with the light. My body resisted attempts to move. My eyelids felt glued shut.

It all ended suddenly when I heard the metallic whirring of a helicopter above my canyon, and a man's voice ask, "Hey, are you that Rosenthal that's out here?" He carried me out of there.

> Credit: Michael Darter

FOOD

4

Not knowing when you'll eat again is among the most primal of human fears. But running out of food in the wilderness is eminently survivable—if you don't let it drive you to make mistakes that cause a real problem. First, humans can survive for weeks without food, and odds are you'll get out long before that. Second, food, after all, is all around you—if you know where to look.

During spring in northern India, the upper Chandra River cuts through a canyon of snow. The sheer-sided snow banks can extend from water's edge to rock walls. As the weather warms, the swollen river erodes the frozen banks, which calve into the icy torrent on one side. On the sunny side of the canyon, the heat melts the snow away from the rock, opening crevasses. In the narrowest spots, a prudent hiker should worry about breaking through on one side or the other. My partner, Ellen, and I had already passed a few such places, and we had no desire to retrace our steps upstream, and then up and over a 15,000-foot pass, to return to the Spiti Valley where we'd started several days earlier. But there's nothing like hunger to cast a new light on formerly unattractive options. In camp, I had unloaded my pack and immediately smelled a problem: Gas had leaked all over our food. I was carrying stove fuel in a cheap plastic container, and gasoline had rendered our lentils inedible.

We salvaged a few biscuits, but we had as much as a week of hiking in front of us—if we could get through at all. We were attempting to trek from Spiti to the Kullu Valley. A dirt track makes the 120-mile journey passable by car in summer, but snow buries it the rest of the year. And an exceptionally deep spring snowpack had delayed even foot travel. We'd seen no one since leaving Spiti, and locals there said nobody had tried the route yet. "Too many avalanches," one said.

Still, we were far from panicked. The human body can survive a long time without food. Irish Republican Army hunger striker Kieran Doherty lasted seventy-three days without eating (at which point he died). In 1992, in Nepal, an Australian trekker got trapped in tricky terrain, in winter, and survived forty-three days on just two chocolate bars and a caterpillar.

So, two days after the fuel spill, after we'd rationed our precious biscuits while hunkered down during a snowstorm that reduced visibility to nil, we still weren't worried about starving. But the hunger pangs were real, as was the uncertainty of the route. What if we kept moving forward, only to get stopped by an impassable section? What if one of us got injured? Would we regret pushing on?

Hunger, it turns out, is scary if there's no end in sight. It's not like fasting, which tests your willpower (don't look in the fridge!), but little else. Not knowing when

➤ Credit: istockphoto

you'll eat again must be among the most primal of human fears, and, unlike some fears, it's not one you'll experience unless the stakes are real. Want to test your fear of heights? There are safe ways you can look over the edge. But you'll never know the deep anxiety of hunger until your body starts to feed on itself—converting glucose and other compounds stored in muscles, the liver, and fat into energy—and you don't know when it will stop.

But here's the trick: Don't let discomfort lead to a real survival situation. Don't make bad decisions because you fear hunger. Don't cross a dangerously high river or forage on potentially poisonous plants or scale a cliff without a rope—all of which can kill more swiftly than an unplanned crash diet.

In India, we knew in our heads we weren't close to starving, even if our stomachs suggested otherwise. On the third day after the fuel spill, we continued along the river, assuming the way ahead would be easier than what lay behind. Rather than dwell on what might go wrong, we joked about making money on our new weight-loss plan.

Soon we arrived at a wide valley with a small, summer farming outpost. The potato farmers hadn't arrived yet, but a caretaker had come to prepare the site. He was thrilled to see us, and insisted we celebrate our successful passage from Spiti with *gurh*, the local moonshine. Between toasts, we tried to tell him what we really needed was food. But he poured another cup and indicated dinner could wait.

Of course, I knew we'd survive a few more hours without a meal. But I nearly died from the hangover. —*BACKPACKER* Editor-in-Chief Dennis Lewon

// EAT OUT: FIND WILD FOOD

The picture of a lone survivor in the wild is typically of a forlorn wraith with skin suctioned to his or her ribs. But in a survival situation, chowing down can wait: Shelter, water, and mental health take priority. Depending on your extra reserves (most of us have them), it takes a month or more to starve to death. Conserve energy and water by staying put rather than foraging. In survival situations, people

> *Dandelions offer easy sources of vitamins and nutrients in almost every part of North America.* Credit: istockphoto

who fast and tap into their inner food stores last 25 percent longer than those who burn calories looking for measly morsels.

But if you can graze on nearby food, that's a bonus. Take a look around: No matter what ecosystem you're in, any survivor is surrounded by the original grocery store. Wherever you are in the world (except Antarctica), your forebears foraged for meals, hunted game, and maybe downed a bug or two right where you stand. It wasn't always easy, but it wasn't a crisis—it was a way of life. With practice, you too can learn to raid nature's pantry, which is full of easily harvested, highly nutritious meals.

Edibles obviously vary widely depending on your location—it always pays to familiarize yourself with an ecosystem's edibles before you visit. But the following are some reliable food sources found in most parts of North America.

Greens

Best Bet: Edible top-to-bottom, dandelions are easy to identify, have sweet flowers, and grow calcium- and vitamin-packed greens (great for salad). Tip: Bitterness increases as plants mature, so boil to reduce bite, or harvest young plants.

Good Choice: Clover provides an iron- and protein-packed meal. Spring shoots and flowers are sweetest; late-fall leaves taste like grass (i.e., not half bad). Tip: The roots have more calories than the greens. Boil leaves and roots to reduce post-snack gut bloat.

In a Pinch: Peppery and full of protein (25 percent of its mass is protein), stinging nettles are edible for careful foragers. Tip: Look up local species, and don't confuse them with other hairy, toxic plants. Eat young shoots and leaves raw; boil mature leaves and roots.

Starches

Best Bet: The "hot-dog-on-a-stick" spiked flowers of cattails are unmistakable. Choice bits: roots (think sweet potato) and white shoots near the root (chop like leeks). Tip: Wash and peel roots to eliminate waterborne pathogens.

HACK THIS: BOIL YOUR GREENS

Give your wild edibles a bath: Boiling can remove bitterness, improve texture and taste, and even remove mild toxins. Timing varies (nettles only need a minute or two), but when in doubt, boil roots, greens, and bitter nuts or seeds (like acorns) for ten minutes, change the water, and boil for another ten minutes. Can't build a fire? Put your produce in a sock, and soak the harvest overnight in a stream.

➤ *Cattail roots provide a solid source of starches when boiled.* Credit: istockphoto

Good Choice: Acorns, though bitter and chalky, are fat- and protein-rich. Tip: Loaded with tannic acid, acorns require processing. You need to soak them for hours or days to avoid stomach upset from tannins before roasting or boiling them (see Hack This: Boil Your Greens on page 98). A cold-water soak will turn brown and tea-like; dump it and keep changing until the water stays clear.

In a Pinch: Cut into pine, spruce, or cottonwood trees to get to the astringent-tasting inner bark. Vitamin C–rich pine is a common and reliable winter food source. Tip: Slice through bark to reach the softest, wettest layer, then peel strips. Chew raw, boil, or fry like chips.

> *Clustered berries almost always offer a safe food source.* Credit: istockphoto

Fruits

Best Bet: Clustered berries grow abundantly, so pick with impunity. All raspberry-style aggregate berries are edible. Tip: Look for productive brambles along the edges of meadows.

Good Choice: Most wooded areas have vast patches of wild rose. Look for red, bulb-shaped rose hips in autumn—you can harvest a hatful of the fiber- and vitamin C–bombs in minutes. Vibrant orange bulbs often survive a few snows. Tip: Split, then scrape out the seeds before chewing the pulpy fruit.

In a Pinch: Thorny hawthorn trees sprout tiny, apple-like fruits; eat the mild fleshy portion and discard the pit (which is poisonous in some species). Tip: All varieties are edible; look for lobed leaves; thorns; and songbirds, which flock to fruiting trees from mid-fall into winter.

Proteins

Best Bet: Fish are nature's jackpot of protein and healthy fats. All North American fresh and saltwater varieties (plus snails, mollusks, and shellfish) are edible. Tip: Bring a fishing kit (see page 107 to make one, and page 121 to improvise one).

Good Choice: Plentiful and nutritious (about half-fat, half-protein), ants and termites are sour but safe to eat (larger bugs contain parasites and/or are often toxic). Tip: Chimp wisdom—poke a stick into an anthill or termite mound to extract the buggers with minimum sting.

In a Pinch: Always cook a grasshopper—it tastes better that way, and you'll avoid inheriting its tapeworms. Tip: Pull off the head, which creates a cavity for spearing it with a roasting stick.

HACK THIS: DESERT FOOD

Arid zones may seem devoid of edibles, but even the dry wastes of the American Southwest offer ample food if you know what to look for.

- **Yucca and agave hearts** are starchy treats, but they require boiling or cooking for hours.
- If you can get past the spines, most **cacti pads** are edible. You can eat them raw, but shave off the spines with a knife and boil or grill them to improve the taste. **Prickly pear fruits** are amazing, and cactus flowers are mildly sweet and offer a burst of fresh moisture.
- Overturn rocks to find **grubs and crickets.**
- **Snakes and lizards** are easiest to catch midmorning, when they're out sunning on rocky ledges.
- Here's the desert delicacy: Many bodies of water—creeks, ponds, even mucky pools—contain **crayfish.**

6 RULES FOR EDIBLE PLANTS

Certain traits help indicate whether a plant may be toxic, including thorns, shiny leaves, umbrella-shaped flowers, white or yellow berries, seed pods, milky sap, an almond scent, and leaves in groups of three. But these signs aren't foolproof, and eating even a tiny bite of a toxic plant can cause extreme gastrointestinal problems, or even death. Happily, survival experts devised a Universal Edibility Test to determine a plant's edibility. When in doubt, follow these steps before chowing down. It's a slow process, but necessary.

> ➤ **Separate the plant into its various parts**—roots, stems, leaves, buds, and flowers. Focus on only one piece of the plant at a time.
> ➤ **Smell it.** A strong, unpleasant odor is a bad sign.
> ➤ **Test for contact poisoning** by placing a piece of the plant on your inner elbow or wrist for a few minutes. If your skin burns, itches, feels numb, or breaks out in a rash, don't eat the plant.
> ➤ If the plant passes the skin test, **prepare a small portion the way you plan to eat it** (boiling is always a good bet).
> ➤ Before taking a bite, touch the plant to your lips to **test for burning or itching.** If there's no reaction after fifteen minutes, **take a small bite**, chew it, and hold it in your mouth for fifteen minutes. If the plant tastes very bitter or soapy, spit it out.
> ➤ If there's no reaction in your mouth, swallow the bite and **wait several hours.** If there's no ill effect, you can assume this part of the plant is edible. Repeat the test for other parts of the plant; some plants have both edible and inedible parts.

Should I Eat Mushrooms?

Short answer: no. Long answer: hell no, unless you're willing to bet your life on it. There are plenty of tasty, edible mushrooms in the woods, and there are loads of disgusting, poisonous mushrooms that look nearly identical to the good ones. Even mushroom foraging experts have to consult their guidebooks and sometimes mis-identify species. The gain is also minimal: Mushrooms contain plenty of vitamins, but they don't offer much by way of calories or protein—the two things you'll need most in a survival situation. Minimize your exposure to risk: Eating a mushroom you feel "pretty good" about is about as dumb as it gets.

➤ *Unless you are an expert, eating mushrooms is almost always risky.* Credit: istockphoto

// HOOKED: SURVIVAL FISHING

Fishing is perhaps the most reliable, safe way to find protein food sources and keep the mind occupied in most wildernesses—whether you're following a mountain stream or lost at sea. Learning the right way to find fish-jumping action, spot streamside sanctuaries, and pull divine meals from pristine waters can make a survival epic feel almost like a vacation. Almost.

On a trip I once took in the North Cascades, our food ran low, but we were surrounded by several large, pristine lakes teeming with trout. (We know because we saw otters catching them.) With little more than string and hooks, we improvised several methods: We dropped fishing lines off dead logs stretching into the lake; we fished actively by casting with an old bottle we discovered; and we even tried to build fish nets. The effort took a few days to pay off, but the reward was worth it: several fat trout, including a stout 17-incher (no big fish story, promise) to ease our hunger.

Now Spear This

To make a fishing spear, find a sturdy stick about 8 feet long and 1.5 inches thick; saplings work well. Split the stick down the center, and make another perpendicular split 6-10 inches long, so you make four prongs (if you have cordage, wrap it just below where you want the split to end to keep it from growing, like in the photo on the next page). Force small sticks along each split to form a cross and splay your points out. Secure them with cordage, if you have it. Sharpen each tip and harden in hot coals for a few minutes. Then pin a fish to the creek bed and grab it with your hands. Spearfishing is notoriously difficult, but try mornings and evenings when insects are hatching near shore.

➤ *An example of a fishing spear.* Credit: Ted Alvarez

String 'Em Along: Make a Trotline

While active fishing with a rod and reel is laid back compared to hunting, learning to fish passively follows a set-it-and-forget-it approach that lets you use energy on other activities, like fire building or shelter making. A simple trotline is one of the easiest ways to do this.

> ➤ Find, make, or scavenge a length of line—paracord works best—that will stretch across a body of water (preferably a stream or river), and leave enough length to tie off on opposite sides of the bank.

> ➤ Attach several droplines with hooks to the paracord, spaced apart at least as far as they are long so they won't get tangled. Number and length can vary depending on the depth and width of the river. If the current is swift, you can tie rocks or other improvised weights on some of the drop lines to keep them low in the water.

> ➤ With your trotline prepared, bait the dropline hooks, and then secure the trotline to opposite sides of the bank (tie the ends to trees, rocks, or sticks driven into the ground).

> ➤ Check the line every few hours for fish, turtles, and even crabs.

> ➤ Tip: If you've got something on the line, make sure not to lift it out of the water: A fish struggling in midair is far more likely to break free. (Speaking from experience, there's nothing more heartbreaking than seeing a

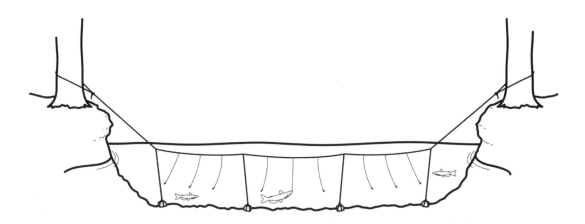

15-pound channel cat break free when you haven't eaten for days.) Pull in the trotline and scoop the fish up at water's edge, or swim out to it and wrap the fish in a piece of clothing. Always get a fishing license and never break local rules unless you are in a true survival situation.

Teach a (Wo)man to Fish

Catching a fish isn't always straightforward or simple (there's a reason "big fish stories" are a thing). Backcountry and survival fishing gets even more complicated, especially when using improvised techniques and tools. Still, acquiring some basic fly-fishing and stalking knowledge before you head into the backcountry will

HACK THIS: PACK A TINY TACKLE BOX

On an extended survival epic, a pocket-size fishing kit could save your life. Luckily, it's a cinch to build. Here's how.

- **Case:** Use an ultralight Altoids Smalls tin (0.5 ounces). Stow it in your pants pocket, in case you lose your pack.
- **Hooks:** Tape at least three hooks of different sizes to the inside of the lid.
- **Line:** Wrap 100 feet of 12-pound line around a business card or pencil.
- **Weights and Lures:** Pack several weights and lures (in case live bait is scarce—or you need to eat the worms yourself).
- **Bobber:** Fit in a mini bobber, or sub a foam earplug.
- **Tweezers:** Tiny tick tweezers make pulling hooks easier.
- **Extras:** Using a larger tin? Squeeze in a mini knife, and more flies, jigs, and line.

➤ *Fish are an excellent food source.* Credit: istockphoto

improve your chances for success. These techniques are best applied to trout and other species that live in mountain lakes and streams.

WATCH FIRST

It helps to see where the fish are biting. If trout are eating on the surface, for instance, try to catch those insects for bait. Look for nymphs on rocks to go after deep-feeding fish. In small streams that lack flying insects, trout eat ants, beetles, spiders, crickets, and other creepy crawlies. If you adventure in trout country, go to a fly-fishing shop and ask for the Parachute Adams and Royal Wulff flies, and pack them in your survival fishing kit—they reliably draw strikes anywhere in the country.

STALK YOUR CATCH

Accustomed to anglers, frontcountry fish often feed in plain sight—making them easy to see and cast to. But fish in high-mountain headwaters are stealthy and skittish. They hide from predators (like hawks) beneath undercut banks, in deep pools, and in the eddies of submerged rocks and logs, which also provide respite from pushy currents. Polarized sunglasses can help you spot them, but don't always rely on a preview of your specific quarry. Use these tricks to find trout and avoid spooking them.

- ➤ **Walk at least 6 feet from the water's edge.** Tracking any closer creates vibrations that put fish on high alert.
- ➤ **Mind your shadow.** Backlight makes fish-spotting easier, but casting a silhouette onto the water scares them into hiding.
- ➤ **Cast from behind natural obstacles** (such as boulders), and crouch low when there's no cover. Sharp-eyed trout can spot tall objects better than short ones.
- ➤ **Drift your bait down currents** that skirt fish hangouts instead of down fast, midstream ones.
- ➤ **Cast across and upstream** to keep your line from landing directly above fish and spooking surface dwellers.
- ➤ **Explore for productive water.** Natural obstacles segregate fish, so some river stretches will be empty while others teem with trout.
- ➤ **Don't underestimate small pools:** An adult trout can live in a desk-size pool in a stream as long as the water is more than 2 feet deep.
- ➤ **Think like a small fish.** Look for logs and rocks that offer hiding spots.

LEARN TO ROLL CAST

Learn to loop or "roll" your line along the water's surface—an essential move where brushy banks prevent a traditional back cast.

- ➤ **Strip out 20 feet of line.** Holding your rod over the water, wave the tip back and forth to feed the line out through the guides.

- ➤ Long casts look nice in photos, but aren't very useful in close-quarters fishing. **Farther than 20 feet will most likely cause problems,** such as casting over fish, which can scare them away.
- ➤ Slowly **lift your arm to a 90-degree angle,** tilting the rod or line (keep your elbow in, hand out) so the line falls beside you. Your thumb should be at forehead level and the rod or line angled at 45 degrees.
- ➤ **Pick a target** and aim your elbow at that spot.
- ➤ **Freeze your arm briefly** (which anchors the line in the water), then rotate your arm from the elbow, accelerating quickly.
- ➤ **Finish by snapping your wrist down,** punching forward with your thumb to accentuate the flick of the line at the end of the cast.
- ➤ **Switch it up:** Practice casting from the left and right sides, which lets you adjust to changing winds.
- ➤ **Troubleshoot your cast.** If your line doesn't fully extend, finish with a stronger wrist snap. If the line collects in the water beside you, keep your elbow high until the final wrist snap.
- ➤ **Don't cast to the same spot** over and over again; the fish will know something is up.

LAND YOUR DINNER

High-mountain fish are usually small enough to reel in without needing to scoop them up in a net or shirt—but you may want to keep one handy just in case (or if you've nabbed a lunker).

- ➤ **Keep the fight in open water** by positioning yourself between your catch and features (like strainers and logs) where it may try to seek refuge.
- ➤ **Follow your catch downstream.** If it takes off, the fish's fight combined with the water's pull may snap your line.
- ➤ If you're using a rod, **keep the tip up** so you maintain a slight bend in the rod to distribute tension along the entire line. A straight rod stresses weak points: the end knots and tippet.

RULES FOR CLEANING FISH

If you didn't learn how to clean a fish at grandpa's knee or in Scouts, chances are you don't know how to do it properly (I certainly didn't). Don't be embarrassed—and don't let it keep you from eating that trout you caught. You can pull off the following with a pocketknife, multitool, or even a sharp stone with a blade at least 3 inches long.

> **Rinse the dead fish** in stream water, vigorously rubbing its skin with your fingers to remove the natural slime layer. Don't bother removing the scales; once cooked, the skin will slip easily from the flesh.

> **Small trout (less than 12 inches) are best gutted and cooked whole.** Grasp the head with one hand, and then cut open the fish's belly from the vent (anus) to the throat, piercing only the skin and leaving the entrails intact.

> *It's messy at first, but gutting a fish gets easy with practice.* Credit: istockphoto

➤ Hold the fish belly up, and **make a second cut just below the lower jaw** and perpendicular to the backbone. Grasp the entrails at the intersection of the two cuts and remove them by pulling toward the tail. Use your knife or thumb nail to scrape out the bloodline that runs along the backbone.

➤ **Large fish (12-plus inches) can be filleted as follows:** (a) Hold the knife parallel to the gill, and slice down to (not through) the backbone. (b) Pivot the blade so it faces the tail and cut along the backbone. Leave the fillet attached to the tail, turn the fish over, and fillet the other side. (c) Cut off the tail and remove any small bones in the fillets.

➤ **Save the guts and nasty bits!** They make excellent bait.

➤ Where bears are a concern, **carry entrails and bones at least a half-mile from camp** and bury them in a cat hole. Wash your hands thoroughly, and change out of your cooking clothes, if you can, or wash them.

COOK AND EAT THE WHOLE FISH

Backcountry fish are often smaller than their frontcountry kin, so filleting can be impractical. Plus, you need every bit of food you can get. Cook fish whole and add a dusting of salt and pepper (the 11th and 12th essentials) for a gourmet campfire meal.

➤ Keep dead fish fresh by placing them in a lake or stream. For the best taste, cook them within two hours of catching and killing them.

➤ To cook without cookware, find a large flat rock (remember, no exploding wet river stones) and tuck it into a nest of blazing hot coals. After a few minutes, throw on your fish, and watch it sizzle until the flesh is flaky and opaque.

➤ You can flip or rotate the fish to ensure even cooking, but if you're worried about losing it, just let it go well done (usually when fins blacken and the meat farthest from the fire flakes or splits).

➤ This isn't the time for sushi: Some fish carry parasites, so make sure it's done. Make sure to have sturdy sticks to retrieve it.

➤ Don't be afraid of the icky bits: Skin, cheeks, eyeballs, and brains taste just like the rest of the fish, only richer. When you're done, boil the carcass to make a fortified broth.

HACK THIS: FISH SKIN GLUE

If you save some fish skin, you can use it to make glue for basic repairs, or to hold together a water vessel. Scrape off the scales, dump the skin in a pot, and add just enough water to cover. Boil until it's the consistency of a sticky syrup. **Note:** It takes a while to set.

// MEAT ME HALFWAY: WILD HUNTING

When Lewis and Clark first crossed into the largely unknown West, their diaries reflected something akin to the Serengeti: millions upon millions of bison, yes, but also unimaginably vast hordes of deer, elk, fowl, and every other type of edible megafauna you can imagine. In any season but winter, the party could scarcely throw a stone without nailing something delicious to eat (beaver tail and bison tongue were favorites). Thanks to the human population's subsequent westward expansion and growth, these wild food stocks are now single-digit percentages of what they once were. But wild game still exists in numbers high enough to sustain a healthy hunting culture into the modern era.

This won't necessarily help you as a beleaguered survivor. As mentioned before, in survival situations active hunting is risky: Burning calories needlessly puts you closer to exhaustion and further from rescue or escape. That said, knowing how to procure wild protein with improvised techniques can build personal confidence in the outdoors, and help win the mental game. In most cases, passive techniques beat active ones: While the idea of traipsing all over the wilderness like Lewis and Clark to bring back dinner seems romantic, the reality of coming back empty-handed with a 2,000-calorie deficit is not. Be smart, and employ these techniques sparingly. Familiarize yourself with hunting rules and regulations, and don't break them unless the situation is life-or-death.

➤ *Wild animals are excellent food sources, if you can catch them.* Credit: istockphoto

Carry a Big Stick

The time and energy it takes to MacGyver arrows, spears, Apache helicopters, etc., makes hunting not worth it. But if you're already out gathering water, foraging, or collecting materials for fire and shelter, Nate Summers of Wilderness Awareness School in Washington state suggests bringing a throwing stick with you. This oldest of hunting tools is lightweight and easy to stow in a pocket or waistband. If you luck into prey in the course of other survival activities, you won't miss the opportunity to take it out.

Look for solid, seasoned (but not rotten) wood about the width of a baseball bat grip and as long as your arm. Longer sticks are easier to use for strikes, but

HACK THIS: SPICE KIT

There's a reason people fought wars over spices: Seasonings go a very long way to making iffy or bland food sources bearable. Any proper survival kit should have a tiny Ziploc full of salt, pepper, and hot chili flakes. Or experiment and create your own all-spice. Capsaicin is key: Even the weak-tongued will pray for a habanero when it comes time to choke down a mouse.

harder to throw. Rabbits and other ground birds and mammals are much harder to kill with a stick than you might think, but it'll work well for lizards and frogs. Summers suggests stalking water edges for waterfowl, which tend to swim out a few feet and slow down once they believe they are safe. They'll still be in stick-throwing range: If you can score a square shot on the body or head (toss it like a tomahawk), or break a wing and swim out to finish the job, congratulations killer! Dinner is duck, duck, goose.

Beware the Snare

Primitive bushcrafting snares, or traps like deadfalls, can be effectively used to capture small-to-medium-size mammals. But they require an immense amount of time and practice to master, and a wide dispersal to yield tiny amounts of food. On a trip on the Mexico-Texas border, I spent two days setting twenty-five Paiute snares (picture the stick-and-rock trap Wile E. Coyote might use) and the effort yielded two measly mice, smashed flat as pancakes. These snare traps also require you to use precious food as bait, and precise knowledge of local fauna behavior and sign. My advice? Skip 'em.

3 RULES FOR A BUG BANQUET

If two billion people can invite insects to the dinner table, it shouldn't be too much of a stretch for you to include edible bugs in your emergency survival diet. Here are some basics to watch out for.

1. **Spot Poisonous Bugs:** While the majority of bugs are safe to eat, plenty aren't. Don't eat any insects that are brightly colored; their coloration is a warning to predators that they're toxic. Avoid hairy bugs; they often hide stingers or the fuzz itself is irritating. Also avoid any bugs that have a potent smell (except, paradoxically, stinkbugs).
2. **Bug Edibility Test:** When in doubt about an insect's edibility, cut off a tiny cooked piece of it, swallow it, and wait a few hours. If no symptoms develop, eat a larger piece and wait again. If nothing happens, it's probably fine.
3. **No Bug Sushi:** Whenever possible, you should cook your insects before you eat them. They may carry parasites or harmful bacteria that cooking will kill, and it improves flavor and makes the nutrients easier to digest.

Bug Buffet

Insects are actually the most abundant protein source on the planet, and many of them boast dense concentrations of omega-3s (the same nutrients that make fish so prized and nutritious). The following crunchy-crawlies are easy to find, nutritious, and have tastes that could plausibly be acquired. You might have to hold your nose or take deep breaths, but, in most cases, you'll be pleasantly surprised at how easy it can be to down a bug. And if you're hungry enough, you won't care. As a friend and sensei once told me before eating a tarantula, "Meat is meat."

GRASSHOPPERS AND CRICKETS

Catch them: Grasshoppers are easiest to catch in the early morning, when they move more slowly. Catch them by hand, or you can trap them by cutting the top off a plastic water bottle (an open Nalgene bottle works, too), burying it in the ground, and dropping in some overripe fruit (if you don't have any fruit, a glow-in-the-dark material like the pull tab from a tent zipper) left overnight works almost as well. Drop in a few leaves so crickets will hide under them instead of trying to escape.

A tossed soda or beer can is never a pretty sight in the wild—but it could be your ticket to a much-needed meal if you find yourself stranded near a body of water. With some floss (or scavenged line), even a child can assemble a simple, usable fishing kit. (**Note:** You can pull off this same technique with a bottle.)

- Measure out several arm lengths of dental floss or line—a minimum of 12 feet or so (depending on the size of your fishing pond).

- Gently squeeze your can in the middle, making it ever so slightly into an hourglass shape. Break off the tab and save it.

- Secure your line to the middle of the soda can with a half hitch or a few fishermen's bends, and begin wrapping it around the middle to make your soda can reel. Leave about 3 feet hanging loose.

- Now grab your tab, and use a multitool to snip an opening in the bottom hole, which will become your hook point. Snip at a steep angle to make it sharp, and use your multitool's file to make it even sharper.

- File or pinch the closed hole of your tab if it has sharp edges so it won't saw through your line.

- Tie your improvised hook to the end of your line.

- Attach live bait, and cast away! Experiment with tying rocks as sinkers and plastic trash (like plastic bottle tops) as bobbers, to help improve your rig. Once you get skilled, you can even spool cast line off the can like a rod and reel (though this works best with a bottle).

> Credit: istockphoto

BROKEN LEG, LOST AND ALONE

BY PAMELA SALANT AS TOLD TO JOSH PRESTIN

// WHEN I CAME TO AFTER I FELL OF THE 50-FOOT CLIFF, I LOOKED AT MY BROKEN AND BLOODY LEGS AND REALIZED THAT I WAS IN BIG TROUBLE.

I was lucky to be alive, but I was alone, without supplies, and no one knew where I was.

I had set out with my boyfriend the previous day to sneak in an overnight while the late-summer Oregon weather was at its finest. Our first choice for a campsite on Mount Defiance was crowded, so we redirected to nearby Bear Lake, a smaller, less popular location with only one established site. But when we reached the lake we were underwhelmed. So we decided to leave our packs on the trail, split up, and search out a prettier, more secluded spot. Of course, it wasn't smart to leave my pack—and map, compass, headlamp, water bottle, everything—behind, but who hasn't done something like that before?

Almost as soon as I left the trail, I got turned around in the thick forest at dusk. I should've called out to my boyfriend, but I didn't believe I could really be lost. Instead, I walked to a high vantage point to reorient myself.

As the last of the light faded, I beat a path back toward the trail. I was scanning for our packs when I stepped right off a ledge and fell 50 feet into a narrow canyon. I heard a snapping sound as I landed legs-first on a pile of rocks, and in the brief moment before I passed out from the pain, I remember one thing: bewilderment.

The next day, the agony was unimaginable. My left leg was broken at the tibia and I could see the bone bulging against the skin. My right leg was covered in sticky, drying blood from a 5-inch-long laceration that needed immediate cleaning. I felt for—and found—a pulse below the break in my left leg. I was relieved since I didn't have splinting supplies close at hand, though splinting would have reduced pain and increased mobility.

I crab-walked 150 feet to the stream in the bottom of the canyon, where I cleaned my wounds with icy snowmelt and drank the unfiltered water. I was lucky it didn't make me sick or infect my open cut, but my wound was filthy, so I took a chance.

I decided to crawl downstream and find help in the Columbia River Gorge, 8 miles northeast. I should have known my boyfriend would go for help, but for some reason I felt compelled to move, however slowly. By pulling myself deeper into the canyon, I was moving out of earshot of the calls of rescuers. I just couldn't calm my mind enough to wait.

As I went, I munched on salmonberries and huckleberries. I figured I was unlikely to starve, but eating gave me a mental boost. I avoided white berries since most of them aren't safe, and looked for aggregate-style berries, such as blackberries and raspberries. I tried to eat a large, brown slug, but it suctioned to my tongue and I coughed it out. I also tried sucking the soupy guts from a caterpillar that left a metallic taste on my lips. I knew to avoid bright colors and hairy bodies, which can indicate the bug is poisonous.

Darkness fell fast in the canyon, and I piled moss over my body to stay warm when temperatures dropped to 40°F. I used pieces of my clothing to keep my laceration covered and clean from debris. Still no one came.

On the third morning, I woke up to the sound of a helicopter. I heard it pass overhead and enthusiastically waved a sock in the air to attract attention. Rescuers reached me by early afternoon, and I recouped in the hospital for a week. I didn't once complain about the food.

➤ Credit: Molly Landreth

NAVIGATION | 5

t starts in your eyes, but you feel it in your guts. The trees get bigger, shadows grow longer, and the whole wild world seems to dilate in preparation to swallow you whole. You are lost. But you can be found—or you can find yourself.

Getting lost in the desert is never an attractive proposition. But it's especially unwelcome in February, when warm days turn suddenly to chilling nights, the light jacket you're wearing is already feeling too thin, and your trail mix is down to just a few raisins.

That's exactly the situation I found myself in during a day hike gone awry in Canyonlands National Park.

A boyfriend and I had set off to hike an 8-mile loop in sunny, perfect, 50°F hiking weather. Right before we left the parking lot, I tossed my puffy down parka back in the car—surely, it was overkill on a day trip. We'd be back in Moab for dinner.

But just a few hours later, we stood facing each other, alternating uneasy glances at the GPS in his hand and the sage-stubbled cliff walls around us. We'd lost the trail in a sandy wash three-quarters of the way through the loop. After thirty minutes of scouting, squinting at the map, and backtracking, we'd made zero progress. There was no denying it: We were really lost.

It was a predicament I'd always worried about but never experienced. But there I was, off-track in the wild and facing exactly that challenge.

I knew what you're supposed to do: return to your last known location. Get back on the established trail. Backtrack if you can or, failing that, stay put so you don't make things worse. Under no circumstances should you go bombing around off-trail.

But now I learned what you really do: panic. Even with all that common sense running through my brain, a deeper instinct pulled me forward, not back. The right path must be close. Just keep moving. Hurry. It'll be fine. I looked at the darkening sky and could almost feel the snowflakes crystallizing in my cells.

Behind us stretched 6 miles of red rock, some of it ice-slicked and steep, and nowhere I'd want to be in the dark. And without a headlamp (of course, neither one of us packed one), turning back seemed like an invitation to disaster. Ahead, somewhere, a trail led a few easy miles back to safety. If only we could find it.

The GPS would save us, right? Wrong. It could tell us where we were, but not how to get to where we wanted to be. We could see the path we sought on the preloaded map, northeast of the little blue dot marking our location. (We'd been

using a simple mapping app as a just-in-case backup, not for careful navigation or recording a track—but now it was all too clear that satellites are no substitute for paying attention.) Could we hike to it through the slickrock maze? The tip of my nose had gone numb by the time we decided to stop looking for our missed junction and just hike cross-country in the trail's general direction. "If we go that way, we should intercept it," my boyfriend said, pointing vaguely into the scrub.

Our plan was to hike in a straight line until we found the trail, but that's easier said than done in canyon country. Side canyons small enough to hide between the topo lines kept cropping up and forcing us off track, twisting me further into disorientation. All the snaking washes behind us looked the same in the twilight, and I realized that we'd passed the point of turning back—even if we wanted to. The fear of being truly lost in that sparkling cold desert made anything but fevered forward motion impossible. I hadn't been so terrified since a lightning bolt struck out of nowhere just as I'd reached 13,000 feet on a New Mexico summit.

Just as the mood went from bad to worse, we scrabbled up a rock wall to find a wide, flat bench. A few more hurried minutes brought us straight to the trail, unmistakable and solid. I practically skipped the last couple of miles to the car, where blasting heat coaxed the blood back into my toes. I would not freeze to death in the desert after all.

Of course, it didn't take long to realize we were probably not in mortal danger from the cold. Temps dropped into the low 20s—uncomfortable for sure, but the weather was dry, so we would have survived. If we'd been stranded overnight where the trail faded out, we could have employed jumping jacks, pacing in circles, sharing body heat. We would've been fine.

Instead, we walked ourselves straight into real danger. Another side canyon or two in the wrong direction on that draining GPS battery, a sprained ankle or a knocked head from slipping on that rock scramble . . .

It was easy to see how hikers get into trouble when they lose the trail. I'd never been lost before, and I was unprepared for the gut-punch of panic it inspired—how losing my place on the map suddenly distorted the friendly wilderness into something menacing. I wanted out of there so urgently that making a decision I knew

was reckless still seemed better than lingering another minute in no-man's-land.
—Elisabeth Kwak-Hefferan, *BACKPACKER* Rocky Mountain Field Editor

// MIND THE MAP: WILDERNESS NAVIGATION

The best way to get found? Don't get lost in the first place. Map and compass are technically mandatory for any adventure, but know how to use them: They're worthless if they just take up pack space. Also, maps get wet, lost, or (ahem) forgotten. Mastering key hacks to navigate without them can make the difference, especially if you know rescue isn't coming.

➤ *Know how to read a map.* Credit: istockphoto

Get a compass, map, and go outside to practice the following lessons—preferably in a place you know well, so you can match your newfound orienteering skills to a familiar environment. When your skills are ready, scale up to practice in a wild place you've never been.

How to Read a Topo Map

A GPS is great, but you should always have a map and know how to use it. Learning how to discern the markings on your two-dimensional map leads to three-dimensional safety. A 7.5-minute topo, on which 1 inch represents 2,000 feet, affords the best terrain detail. Here's a guide, with indicators overlaid on a topo map and real life features.

Contour Lines: Each thin, brown line represents a single elevation. Check the bottom corner of your map for the contour interval, which tells you how many vertical feet apart they are from one another (usually 40 feet). Thicker lines, or "index lines," are labeled with the elevation in feet.

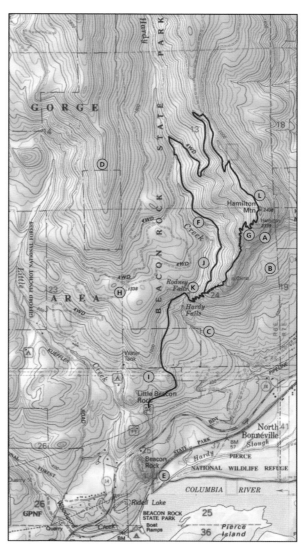

➤ Credit: Melissa Baker

Below are the various parts of the map to know. Match up the letters below with the letters on the map (p. 128).

A. **Steep terrain:** crowded sections of contour lines

B. **Gradual terrain:** spacious sections of contour lines

C. **Gully:** V-shaped contour lines "point" toward higher elevations

D. **Ridge:** V-shaped contour lines "point" to lower elevations

E. **Cliff:** super-concentrated lines

F. **Trail:** black, dashed line

G. **Switchbacks:** zigzagging trail

H. **Dirt road:** black, dashed double-line

I. **Railroad tracks:** solid black line with hatch marks

J. **Stream:** solid blue line

K. **Waterfall:** single blue hatch intersecting a stream

L. **Summit:** contour line forms a small circle

➤ Credit: Melissa Baker

How to Read a Compass

Mastered the map? Good. But you won't know where you are or where you're going unless you can use a compass, too. This indispensable piece of technology has served the wayward on land and sea for centuries (some credit its invention to the ancient Chinese, others to medieval Venetians). Master the compass and get one step closer to becoming a bona fide explorer—or just a competent outdoorsperson. Here's how.

TAKE A BEARING OFF THE MAP

You want to travel from Peak A to Peak B. Lay the edge of the compass on the line between the two landmarks on the map, with the direction of travel arrow pointing from A to B. Turn the housing until the compass's meridian lines are parallel to the map's longitude lines. (Make sure the "N" on the housing points toward the top of the map.) The index mark indicates the true bearing—but not exactly the bearing you want to follow. To find that, you have one more step.

➤ Credit: AJ Cann/Flickr

CORRECT FOR DECLINATION

The needle points to magnetic north, not true north, and they're hundreds of miles apart. Because topographic maps are oriented to true north, you need to resolve this difference, called declination. It's especially important when you're traveling long distances off trail. The fix is all math. Subtract the declination from your compass bearing for west, and add it for east. Of course, everyone forgets this when it counts, so remember this mnemonic: Maps Tell Almost Everything. Translation: Magnetic to True Add East. Yes, you can buy a compass with a "set and forget" declination function so you can skip the math for each bearing, but you should still understand how it works. Look for declination on the lower left portion of your topo map; you'll see two diverging lines with the angle listed between them. If it says "16 degrees east," rotate the compass housing so the magnetic north/compass needle mark sits 16 degrees to the right (east) of the true north orienting lines. Twist the screw to reach the proper orientation. You can also usually find declination for a given area online.

USE THE RIGHT MODEL

Historically, compasses were made for either the Northern or Southern Hemisphere (with needles balanced to compensate for varying magnetic pull). Such location-specific models are still sold widely (they're cheap and effective), but plenty of brands make global compasses with needles that work everywhere.

AVOID METAL

Don't spread the map on the car hood at the trailhead and then put your compass on the map. Metal interferes with the magnetic needle.

FIND YOUR LOCATION

Lost? If you can see two or more known landmarks separated by at least 45 degrees, you can triangulate—zero in on—your position. Plot their bearings, and where they cross is your location. Don't forget to correct for declination.

HACK THIS: EMERGENCY COMPASS

Show off your survival IQ with this emergency compass: Rub a needle with a magnet, set it on a floating leaf, and it'll point north. Keep a magnetized needle in your first aid kit and use this party trick if cloud cover eliminates help from the stars, sun, and moon.

FOLLOW A BEARING

With the compass set to your intended direction of travel, hold it level and turn until the red or arrow end of the north-seeking needle (often called "red Fred" in compass class) is in the "red shed" on the housing. Now pick the most distant identifiable tree or landmark you can see that lies on your bearing and hike to it. Repeat.

Navigate in Poor Visibility

In darkness, fog, or dense vegetation, you've encountered a worst-case scenario: Traditional line-of-sight route-finding won't work. But these three strategies can keep you on track.

1. **Preload a GPS.** Preloaded maps, tracks, and waypoints go far in giving you more data to work with. Before a trip, program intermediate waypoints to guide you through safe zones, mark hazards like cliffs or steeps, and show locations of bailouts or shelters that might be helpful in an emergency. With a map in hand–even if you forgot to preload your GPS with relevant data–you can input UTM coordinates if on-trail conditions deteriorate. You can find UTM (Universal Transverse Mercator) coordinates and latitude/longitude coordinates in the margins of most topo maps.

2. **Follow short sight lines along your bearing.** When visibility is good, you'd use a compass (or your GPS unit's compass screen) to identify landmarks near your destination, which may be many miles away. In low visibility you

➤ *In low visibility, travel along a steady elevation.* Credit: istockphoto

can do the same thing, but with shorter distances. Stay attuned to your surroundings; don't follow your GPS screen blindly into a dangerous situation. Take short "sight lines" to align close-in, visible features with your desired bearing. Hike between the features and when you reach the more distant target, use your compass to identify another landmark along the bearing. Continue leapfrogging benchmarks toward your destination.

3. **Travel along landmarks.** You can still use landscape contours to guide travel when peaks, valleys, or navigation handrails—easy-to-follow landscape features like ridges or the tree line—aren't visible. Identify a safe travel zone based on an elevation range and use your GPS or altimeter to stay within that range as you hike. Be aware that uncalibrated altimeters may have a 100-foot margin of error. Improve your unit's accuracy by 50 percent or more by calibrating it every time you turn it on.

HACK THIS: NAVIGATE OFF-TRAIL

Fact: The vast majority of wilderness isn't even crossed by a trail. Here's how to make your way safely across the big empty.

FIND THE EASIEST WAY AROUND

- **Follow game trails.** In overgrown areas frequented by large species, follow animal paths to increase your pace. Climb or descend by stair-stepping between trails, which often run parallel across slopes.
- **Skirt vegetation.** Avoid dense flora in wetlands and draws. Instead, travel on ridgelines or above tree line, if possible. In general, vegetation is thicker on northern and windward slopes.
- **Contour around hills.** Save energy by navigating hillsides along one elevation (use your GPS altimeter). Contour lines on maps may not expose impassable cliffs or other hazards, so look ahead to avoid tough or dangerous terrain.

STAY ON COURSE AND USE THE LAND TO GUIDE YOU

- **Follow a handrail.** Identify your target (X) and a linear feature that leads toward it, like a stream or ridge, on your map. Guide your direction of travel by hiking parallel to this handrail until you're near your goal.
- **Reference a nearby land feature.** Identify a prominent landmark within half a mile of your target destination, like a lake. Hike to that point via the easiest route and then use your map and compass to fine-tune a bearing and calculate the distance to your goal.

➤ *Even without a map or compass you can orient yourself.* Credit: istockphoto

// MAPLESS: IMPROV NAVIGATION

It happened: You forgot your map and compass, or you lost them. This is not ideal, but you can find a way through with some time-tested, improvised navigational tools and techniques.

1. **Orient Yourself:** Start by locating the sun. It rises in the east and sets in the west (yes, lost persons have messed this up). It also sits low on the southern horizon during winter and, by midsummer, is almost overhead. If the time is close to noon, use this watch method to fix a direction more accurately:

Take an analog watch (or draw one on the ground, taking the time from your digital watch). Position the watch so the hour hand points at the sun. The line that bisects the angle between the hour hand and 12 o'clock (1 o'clock during daylight saving time) is aligned north to south; find north by recalling that the sun tracks through the southern horizon.

2. **Find the North Star:** At night, you can identify Polaris (the North Star) by first finding the easily recognized Big Dipper. Take the two stars that form the lip of the Big Dipper's cup, and trace a line upward (for about five times the distance between the two stars) until you reach a faint star. This is Polaris, and it always points north. Mark this direction in the dirt before sheltering for the night, and in the morning use it to set your direction.

3. **Backtrack:** Stop moving, and start thinking about your last known location, usually a singular spot like a summit, trail sign, river crossing, or a lake. Return to that place if possible. If you can't backtrack, you'll need to navigate by dead reckoning. The good news is that most hikers lose their way within a mile of a marked trail, road, parking lot, or structure. If you know a road or a trail is somewhere east of your location—and you're certain you can travel east without a compass—head in that direction. The bad news is that

HACK THIS: FINDING NORTH WITH A STICK

Use the stick-and-shadow method: When the sun is casting shadows, place a 3-foot stick vertically into the flat ground. Clear the area around it of debris. Mark the tip of the stick's shadow with a stone. Wait for at least 15 minutes and mark the end of the shadow again. The line connecting the marks roughly coincides with the east-west line. A line perpendicular to this line through the central stick indicates the north-south line.

lost people generally cannot follow a straight line across wilderness terrain. Once again: Unless you are totally confident, stay put, and wait for rescue.

4. **Check Often:** If you're lost, regularly double-check your direction as you hike to make sure you're not wandering in circles or letting the terrain determine your path.

How to Navigate with Stars

Sailors have used these techniques for centuries—and on clear nights you can, too, provided you're in the Northern Hemisphere. The night sky offers different

▶ *Don't get distracted by the majesty: The North Star can help you navigate by night.* Credit: istockphoto

constellations down south, so southern-latitude adventurers must familiarize themselves with an entirely different array of celestial signs, which we won't go into here.

FIND NORTH

First, find Polaris, or the North Star, which lies almost directly above the north celestial pole. You'll locate Polaris straight out from the tip of the Big Dipper's bowl, almost as if it were being poured from the giant ladle. As mentioned before, trace a line upward from the two stars that form the lip of the Big Dipper's cup about five times the distance between said two stars until you reach Polaris, which is fainter than you'd probably imagine. If you hit the constellation Cassiopeia—which is shaped like a W—you've gone too far.

If the Big Dipper isn't visible (it could be obscured by clouds, or terrain when it's low on the horizon), you can still find Polaris by following a line bisecting the wider V of Cassiopeia. Polaris is also the end of the handle on the Little Dipper. Once you find it, let your eyes fall to the point on the horizon directly below. This will be close to due north. **Tip:** You can find Polaris in the night sky using your fist if you know your current latitude. Example: Denver lies at about 40 degrees latitude. Your clenched fist at arm's length represents about 10 degrees. So if you face north near Denver and outstretch your arm, you should find Polaris somewhere to the north about four fists high.

FIND SOUTH

If the moon is a crescent and high in the sky, connect the tips of the crescent. Find where the line hits the horizon—that's south. If Orion is high in the sky and his sword is close to vertical, the point where the line made by the sword would hit the horizon also points you south. (*Note:* Both of these methods yield rough estimates compared to finding north with Polaris, which is highly accurate.)

SAVE YOUR DIRECTION

If you're using one of these methods to orient yourself but will wait for daylight to hike, draw an arrow in the dirt (or use rocks or sticks) so you don't go astray come morning.

TELL TIME

Imagine a giant clock in the sky, with the line you drew connecting Polaris and the Big Dipper as the hour hand. This clock is a little different than your average analog—it's a 24-hour clock, and it runs counterclockwise. On March 6, when the line points due north at midnight, it's perfectly accurate. In any other month, take the number of months after March 6, multiply it by two, and subtract it from the time you read (don't forget to add an hour during daylight saving time). For example, if the hour hand points to 7 a.m. on July 21, subtract 8 to reach 11 p.m. Add one more hour to account for daylight saving and read the correct time (midnight.) If the Big Dipper isn't visible, you can use Cassiopeia. If using Cassiopeia, the line that connects the tip of the narrow V and Polaris is your new hour hand, and the perfectly accurate day to remember is March 21.

// VITAL SIGNS: ALERTING RESCUERS WITH SIGNALS

When you're lost or injured, you need a foolproof way to get your rescuers' attention. If you left your itinerary with a responsible adult, someone will be looking for you when you don't return. Help them find you by using the three basic types of signals: reflection, light, and sound.

Sound

Making noise might be the most versatile way to attract attention. Loud sounds, such as whistles, can reach long distances at any time of day and can alert would-be rescuers to your location when you can't otherwise be seen. The drawback is they can't travel as far as sight. Here are three options.

Loudest: The Storm safety whistle (0.7 ounces; stormwhistles.com) lives up to its billing as the "world's loudest." My testing registered 107 decibels (comparable to a car horn) and the tone carried a third of a mile on a blustery day. Bonus: Weak puffs produce shrieks—a plus for injured hikers.

▶ *Be loud, be seen: It may take repeated attempts to notify rescuers to your location.* Credit: istockphoto

Best Buy: Cheap and light whistles like Fox 40's Classic Safety (0.5 ounces; fox40world.com) are as loud as a power mower up close (103 decibels) and audible up to a quarter-mile. The pea-less design works when waterlogged. Warning: Loud alerts require full lung capacity.

DIY: A practiced talent can easily reach the upper-90-decibel range with a two-fingered wolf whistle. (The world record is an air-horn-like 125 decibels.) Practice it: Tuck your lips over your teeth, insert two fingers into your mouth (angled inward), position your tongue behind your lower teeth, and exhale sharply.

Reflection

There's a reason survival mirrors are a recommended part of any survival kit. Using just the power of the sun, stranded hikers can flag down help from miles away.

HACK THIS: CELL PHONE SIGNALING

Lost with nothing but your phone? Use it to get rescued.

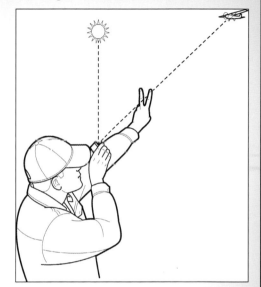

- Text your last known location, condition, and SOS to your entire address book.
- Call 911. Emergency calls will go through if detected by any network.
- Preserve batteries. Turn your phone on for five minutes a day to seek reception.
- Flash a signal with the screen. Hold your fingers in a V-shape at arm's length, pointed at your target. Tilt the phone until the screen reflects light at the V; rotate it so the light alternates between your fingers, flashing your target.

Caveats: Mirrors don't work at night or without direct sunlight, and they take a little practice to use.

Flashiest: Coghlan's 3-by-2-inch glass mirror (2.2 ounces; coghlans.com) flashed spotters from 2.5 miles away, and survivalists say it's visible from 20 miles in good conditions. The glass is scratch resistant, and the sight enables pinpoint aiming. Ounce-counters: Try AMK's SOL Rescue Flash Mirror (0.4 ounces; adventuremedicalkits.com).

7 RULES FOR GETTING FOUND

If you're lost in the wilderness, you can boost your chances of getting home—or you can become your own worst enemy. Here's how to aid rescuers in finding you safe and sound.

1. **Stay calm.** When you think you're lost, stop and have some water and a snack. This prevents rash decision-making.

2. **Retrace your footsteps.** This strategy comes with a caveat: You have to admit when you're just plain lost and then stop. Dead reckoning back to where you think the trail is wastes time and energy. Try to recall landmarks you can use to pinpoint your location on a map. Consider your supplies, and the skills and resources of group members. Are there imminent hazards, like lack of water or changing weather? If you can backtrack safely, do it.

3. **Don't wander off-trail hoping it'll "just work out."** If you're confident in backtracking, do it in the daylight and allow plenty of time to find shelter and water before dark. Check your direction of travel often, and mark your path with rocks or sticks in case you lose your way again.

4. **Use your map.** With decent map skills in open terrain, you can locate yourself.

5. **But don't "bend the map."** Disoriented hikers may fall into the trap of telling themselves their surroundings match what's on their map, even when they don't. Look at the terrain first, then try to find what you're seeing in the topo lines, not the other way around. Likewise, trust your GPS and compass— they're usually right.

6. **Stay put.** If someone has your itinerary and will alert rescue authorities when you don't check in, wait in a safe place. Search-and-rescue (SAR) teams often sweep certain areas then move on. By wandering, you risk entering an area they've already cleared.

7. **Be obvious.** Setting fires, signaling with a mirror, hanging shiny objects on trees, and blowing a whistle can broadcast your position to nearby rescuers. Leave signs if you must move to stay safe, or if you seek higher ground to signal for help.

DIY: No mirror? When buffed with a little spit, the shiny inside of a snack wrapper caught enough rays to alert spotters over a mile and a half away. Aiming is hard; pull the wrapper tight and wave it overhead like crazy. Repeat.

Light

Bright lights might be your best bet for getting spotted once the sun sets. New lasers can capture attention from extreme distances (careful; they're illegal to shine at aircraft in some places), but even headlamps and camera flashes work from miles away.

Brightest: Greatland Rescue's Laser Light (2.3 ounces; greatlandlaser.com) is a shotgun slug-size signaling bazooka. The beam sweeps a fan of light (easier to aim

HACK THIS: BY A CELL PHONE

Live Phone: If you don't have signal, keep your phone off to save battery except for one five-minute window per day. Even with little or no signal you can ping a nearby tower and leave a trail for rescuers to follow. Head to high ground to improve reception. If your battery is low, text emergency contacts—texts require less power and can transmit over a weaker connection than a voice call. Texting to 911 does not work in all areas.

Dead Phone: Use the metallic, mirror-like layers behind the screens inside your phone to flash a distress signal. Most phone speakers contain magnets, and all phones contain many little wires that can be magnetized to serve as an improvised compass. Not all wires work—test it to see which one is attracted to the magnet. Use those same wires to ignite dry tinder by touching them to the positive and negative terminals of the battery to create a red-hot poker. Abrade the circuit board against a rock to create a cutting edge, and shape it into a point. Use the remaining parts to create fishing hooks and lures.

than a pinpoint) that caught a spotter's eyes like lightning from 7 miles away in my tests (the manufacturer claims a 20-plus-mile range).

Multiuse: An ordinary 35-lumen LED headlamp outperformed a flare and survival strobe—with zero extra ounces or cost. My spotters saw an SOS clearly from 2 miles, and the strobe option lit up a tester's position (in tree cover) from a mile. The

SAVED BY: A KNIFE

If you can only have one survival tool, make sure it's a strong and sharp knife. It's the one tool that can do everything—from signaling for help to starting a fire to catching your dinner. A single, fixed blade excels at hard-duty wood work, which true survival situations often demand. A folding blade is more compact, but shouldn't be more than a backup. In a fixed-blade knife, you want the blade metal to extend all the way through the handle in one continuous piece (called full tang). This increases durability and strength.

Serrated blades are good for sawing fibrous materials or cutting bone, but are harder to sharpen. Choose a synthetic grip that fits your hand and

doesn't slip when wet. Avoid handles that store things (which means the knife doesn't have a full tang). Get a stainless or carbon steel blade, about 3 to 6 inches long (avoid getting into Rambo territory). Stainless resists rust better; carbon is easier to sharpen in the field. Daggers are not for hikers: A single cutting edge allows you to use the spine (make sure it's flat) for techniques like fire-starting and splitting wood by hammering on the flat edge.

CARVE A FUZZ STICK
Increasing a stick's surface area helps it grow a small flame. Snap a dead, thumb-thick branch off a downed tree. Listen for a cracking sound, which signals the branch is dry (touch the broken end to your lips to confirm). Starting from the bottom, carve in at 30 to 35 degrees to peel back shavings of wood, creating an umbrella effect. Continue until the entire stick is fuzzed.

> Credit: istockphoto

diffuse beam blunts accuracy; go to a clearing for maximum reach. Triple-A battery power averages sixty to eighty hours.

DIY: Brought your camera, but no light? A pop-up DSLR flash can effectively signal spotters from 2 miles. Triggering an SOS might be impossible, but three successive flashes followed by several minutes of darkness still signals an alert. Save it for when rescuers are searching and you can spot them; flashing drains battery power.

MAKE A WEAPON

To fashion a spear, use your knife to split an inch-thick stick about 6 inches at one end, then tie your knife into place with cordage. Style points: Fasten the knife perpendicular to the stick to make a tomahawk.

MAKE A BOW

To make a primitive bow strong, you must follow a single growth ring for the entire length. (Crossing the wood grain weakens the bow.) For that you need a planing technique. Try this: Hammer a plug of wood onto the point of a fixed-blade knife. Using both hands, draw the knife toward you carefully at a 90-degree angle to the wood to refine imperfect branches into bows, arrows, or snowshoes.

SCRAPE OUT A BOWL

Use hot coals to burn a bowl out of a log. Hold your blade at 90 degrees to the work surface and scrape out the char to finish your vessel.

PROCESS FIREWOOD

Wish you had an axe for splitting bigger wood to feed a fire or make a shelter? Set the knife's edge where you want to "chop," then use a heavy object—like a rock or a small log—to hammer the spine of the knife.

SIGNAL HELP

Spit-shine your blade as clean as you can and buff it until it gleams. To aim, create a V with the fingers of your outstretched, non-dominant hand and center your target (aircraft, ground searchers) in the V. Hold the knife close to your chest, playing with

angles until you catch the sun. Now, flash the target in the V of your fingers (the V gives you visual confirmation that your effort is working).

STAY SHARP

A sharp knife should easily slide through a piece of paper. If yours doesn't, get to work with a whetstone (at home). Got a dull blade in the field? Find a smooth, palm-size stone (river rocks work well). Add spit. Place your blade at about a 15-degree angle to the stone, and apply gentle pressure as you swipe the blade over the stone in a smooth, fluid, arc-like motion. Make about thirty passes, then flip the blade over and do the same on the other side.

LOST AND BLIND IN THE WOODS

BY KENNETH KNIGHT
AS TOLD TO CAROLYN WEBBER

// THE BLAZES GUIDING HIKERS ALONG THE APPALACHIAN TRAIL (AT) HELP MOST PEOPLE, BUT NOT ME.

I can't see them until they are a foot or so away because I'm legally blind. I have one eye and can't make out details a few feet away without a monocular. Still, I live to explore new places and enjoy rare experiences just as much as the next hiker.

There were seven of us setting out in April on a 60-mile backpacking trip along the Appalachian Trail from Petites Gap to Peaks of Otter Lodge in Virginia. It was something of a homecoming for me. Even with my vision as it is, I've hiked almost 1,700 miles of the AT—and even completed this section before, only south to north. This trip was also a test run for an even bigger adventure—the 180-mile cross-country Great Outdoor Challenge that I would be doing in Scotland in a month.

I had everything I needed to hike independently: my backpack, a 30°F sleeping bag, a mountaineering tent, several layers of clothing, a map, and dehydrated food to last me the week.

I met the other hikers in an online hiker's forum, and our loose relationships led to a loose dynamic on the trail. The group ebbed and flowed in size as we meandered through the dense hardwood forest. Some days I walked with the others, sometimes I went alone. Because of my blindness, every step was cautiously placed, especially when on rolling, rocky terrain. Going at my own slower pace suits me, but our group always agreed to meet at the end of the day.

About halfway through our trip, I was solo hiking when I must have stepped onto a game trail.

I don't remember the moment, but I remember stopping and allowing the severity of my situation to sink in. I had no idea where I was. The trail was gone, and heavy leaf litter hindered every attempt to draw some useful clue from the ground that would help me.

I walked back and forth, hoping to intersect the trail. After twenty minutes, I gave up. It was no use, just repetitive forest in all directions. At this point, I didn't know how far from the trail I'd strayed or in which direction. I tried to stay calm, reassuring myself I'd be OK. I knew there is seldom water on the AT itself in that section, and I didn't want to hunker down and wait without water if I wasn't sure I'd hear somebody if he or she walked past on the trail. So I made the choice to head generally downhill to where I knew the James River would be, in hopes that I'd cross one of its tributaries. After about an hour of picking my way steeply downhill, I heard gurgling. I filtered water, drank deeply, and rested, considering my options.

Just as everyone tells you to do when lost, I decided to stop and wait for someone to find me. Surely, once my fellow hikers realized I wasn't at the meeting point, they would alert the US Forest Service and local sheriff's office. I had enough food for a few days and access to water, so, once I found a spot for my tent, I settled in.

I made myself visible by hanging an emergency blanket in the trees. I explored my surroundings to see if I could find a trail, but I never went far; I was nervous to lose my camp. Plus, the terrain was rocky and steep, and a misstep could mean injury. I rationed my food—about three days' worth of dehydrated meals—and made signal fires.

Missing Rescue

Day two passed, then day three. I began to wonder if a search party was actually coming.

Though my stress increased with each passing day, the weather was mild, and I was OK. Each morning, I packed up all my gear—so I had it with me in case I couldn't find my way back—and explored a new direction. I was hopeful I'd find a way out, but my fear of getting lost or injured kept me from venturing more than a quarter mile from my camp, which sat on a knoll that I'd marked with cairns of rocks and twigs to guide me back.

Returning unsuccessful, I ate my daily meal, set up camp, and lit another signal fire. Mostly, I waited. It was monotonous, but I knew it was my best chance of survival. Even traipsing around my camp, I managed to get bruises and scrapes. Risking injury or losing my camp with my dwindling food rations was not an option.

Day four passed, then day five. *Maybe the rescue team isn't coming after all*. If no one was on the way, I'd have to save myself. I started planning my escape. I figured that if I followed the stream, it would eventually lead to the James River, and from there I could hopefully find a trail, a road, or a home.

Tomorrow will be the day. If no one comes to get me tomorrow, I am getting out myself.

I awoke depressed on my sixth day alone. I was hungry, my food was gone, and no one was coming. In a last-ditch effort to be found, I cleared some land to make a bigger fire (but not so big that I couldn't easily put it out) and planned my exit.

A few hours later I heard someone, and I will never forget the joy I felt. A team of firefighters approached the camp, looking for the blaze. They found me, too. (They weren't part of the rescue effort.) I told them I'd been lost. A couple of them put out the fire while others helped me pack up for the final time. I was thrilled to be with people who knew where we were. In just 200 yards, we reached a hunting trail and, thirty minutes later, we came to a trailhead.

Though hungry, I was mostly just relieved. As it turned out, my hiking group thought we were meeting at the end. When they finished, they realized something was wrong and called for help. About 130 searchers were out looking for me, but they'd only started two days earlier. Waiting was the hardest part.

▶ Credit: Peter Baker

FIRST AID | 6

Maybe you were careful, maybe you weren't. But the worst happened: injury. A fall, an animal, an exploding camp stove. Forget the causes: You or someone you love is left a broken, bloody mess. Help is on the way, but the "help" in this case is you—if you can stay calm and summon the grit and knowledge to treat injuries both mundane and catastrophic.

I once knew a guy—an inexperienced hiker—who went out for an overnight on the Appalachian Trail, got left behind by his hiking buddy, and panicked. A trail runner found him fifteen minutes later, broken, blubbering, and gearless on a blue-blaze trail. He'd ditched his pack because he thought it would slow his escape. He was crying because he wasn't ready to die. That's not survival. Sprained your ankle and forced to hobble out using a tree branch for a crutch? That's not survival either. That's a mishap, a blip, a frightening but ultimately funny story.

So what is survival? You'll know when the real thing happens because, if you come back at all, you come back without something dear to you. Maybe it's a finger, or a friend, but more likely something that was once glued to your psyche, so close you never realized it was there: the belief that the world is forever filled with warm beds, warm partners, and happy endings for all the pretty much good-enough people like you. Survival changes that. It cleaves your life in two: before it happened and after it happened. And in the middle is a gigantic monument that casts a shadow from which you may never emerge.

You'll know survival is at stake when you find your faith. Then lose your faith. You will stare your own mortality in its pale and hollowed-out face, and if that image doesn't stalk you by day, you can count on seeing it in your dreams.

Such life-or-death situations can materialize out of the night and set upon you. But more likely, they're the final step in a series of bad calls that forced you—at the knife point of stupidity—past the place where you can get back to being normal, or happy, or warm. Your sprained ankle, say, makes you eager to find a shortcut home. You cut switchbacks, you follow animal trails, because you just know you're almost there. Then, in a flash of noise and motion, you're lying at the bottom of a small cliff, ears filled with the whine of adrenaline, pounding heart, and gasping breaths.

You'll know what's at stake when you realize that the world, with all its near-infinite beauty, doesn't give a damn about your good times, your feelings, or your sense of fairness.

Of course, you've always known that—in an airy, detached sort of way—because you've heard about it happening to other people and you've thought to yourself, *I'm too smart / prepared / careful for that*. But now, for the first time ever, you'll feel it—subtle as a rasping and unanswered scream for help—right down into your bone marrow. That is survival. And then you'll know it's time to get to work. —*BACKPACKER* Deputy Editor Casey Lyons

// ACT FAST: ESSENTIAL FIRST AID TIPS

Before you let the fear of outdoor injury overwhelm you, it's important to remember you're more likely to fatally injure yourself in your bathtub than on the trail. On average, just 160 visitors die in national parks per year—and visitation topped 331 million visitors in 2016. Sure, spraining your ankle could leave you stranded and vulnerable, but only a few traumas are serious enough to kill on their own. Still, should a potentially fatal injury occur, you'll want to have mastered the basics of backcountry first aid—and, even if it isn't fatal, memorizing a few tricks can promote rescue and ease discomfort. The following first aid tips are in descending order of seriousness and likelihood.

Note: While the information sourced here comes from medical and search-and-rescue (SAR) professionals, it is in no way a substitute for proper medical treatment and is intended for informational purposes only. Let's get to it, then.

Head Injury: Brain Check

It doesn't take a lot to scramble your nerve center. Falls with momentum (skiing, mountain biking) and from a height (climbing, scrambling) are most dangerous, but even short tumbles can rattle your noggin enough to cause problems. The brain sits just a millimeter away from the inside of the cranium, so a hard enough blow can knock it around inside your skull like a ping-pong ball, resulting in bleeding or swelling that could do you in. A swollen, injured brain presses against the skull,

> *Treat all injuries seriously and evacuate the victim if he or she loses consciousness or responsiveness.*
Credit: istockphoto

eventually squeezing shut blood vessels and starving the tissue of oxygen. That's only if the mounting pressure doesn't squish your brain stem first, pulling the plug on your heart and lungs.

Treat all blows to the head seriously and evacuate if the victim loses consciousness or responsiveness, even for a minute. Look for a headache, vision problems, dizziness, disorientation, and nausea/vomiting. Signs of a more severe brain injury include loss of coordination, combativeness, and fluid leaking from the nose, mouth, or ears. If symptoms are mild and the victim has no spine injury, you can give acetaminophen for a headache and walk him or her out to treatment. If you suspect there's an additional spine injury or symptoms are severe, hike to or call for immediate rescue.

➤ *Get help to evacuate the victim as soon as possible.* Credit: istockphoto

Spine: Protect Your Neck

Once again, falls (especially from more than twice your height, and especially involving speed) are the common culprit for this dead-serious injury. The spinal cord acts as a switchboard connecting all your body systems to your brain. Sever it completely, especially at the neck, and breathing might stop altogether. Fortunately, your hard bones make this very difficult to do. More likely, you'll pinch or bruise the spinal cord and cause permanent paralysis and the loss of bladder and bowel control, sensation, and the ability to breathe on your own. (Still horrifying.) The neck's smaller vertebrae and lack of support make it particularly vulnerable—so think twice about that show-off backflip.

After a fall, don't let a victim move before assessing him or her for spine injury: Signs include sharp pain in the neck or spine when touched, a tingling sensation in

the hands and feet, weakness, and paralysis. If you suspect an injury, it's critical to immobilize the person's neck and backbone.

Have someone kneel at the victim's head and hold the neck still. You can also improvise a cervical collar out of a bulky, rolled-up layer of clothing or a trimmed foam sleeping pad held in place with tape. Or use an empty internal frame backpack as a makeshift splint for the spine. Place it under the victim, bottom by his or her head, and buckle the hip belt over his or her forehead, cinching until firm. (Make sure to keep the person's head, shoulders, and hips aligned when sliding the pack under him or her. This isn't easy: Practice at home, or take a wilderness first aid course to practice this maneuver.) Keep the victim still, and call for help; the only safe way out is on a rigid litter (stretcher) with trained rescuers.

Internal Bleeding

You fall on rocks, or a rock (or tree) falls on you, causing blunt trauma to the abdomen. Uh-oh: Solid organs like the liver (as opposed to hollow ones like the stomach) bleed when ruptured, causing swelling within the injured organ (bad) or spilling blood into the abdomen (worse). This is especially worrisome when it happens to the aforementioned liver, which holds 13 percent of the body's blood at any given moment, and the spleen, another serious bleeder. If the internal tear is big enough, you can bleed out in minutes.

Inspect the injured area for bruising and pain when touched. Check the victim's pulse: A pulse that remains elevated twenty to thirty minutes after the impact, along with rapid breathing and pale, wet skin, indicates internal bleeding. Keep the victim still and call or hike for a rescue. A skyrocketing pulse means get a helicopter, yesterday.

Splint Anything

Sticks and stones can break your bones, and in the backcountry, they often do. Knowing how to stabilize and protect a break or sprain can help reduce pain and further injury until help arrives—or give you the best shot at hiking out when no one's coming for you. Here's how to splint and secure almost everything that can break.

➤ *Know how to stabilize a break or sprain.* Credit: Caveman Collective

UPPER ARM

1. Pad the outer arm with base- or mid-layers.
2. Fasten a humerus-length (about 10-inch) trekking pole, stick, or tube of foam pad to it using socks, duct tape, webbing, etc.
3. Improvise a sling: Place the hand of the injured arm over the chest. Slide a base layer underneath so the wide part cups the elbow and tie behind the shoulder. Secure the sling to the body with another layer.

ANKLE

1. Tape an anchor. Wrap a piece of duct tape around the leg 2 inches above the anklebone. Keep it snug, but not so tight that it cuts off circulation.
2. Attach stirrups. Position the foot at a 90-degree angle to the leg, and tape it in place with three overlapping stirrups—they go under the arch and up to the anchor. Secure in place by adding another piece of tape over the anchor.
3. Stabilize sway. From the inside anchor, wrap underneath the arch and over the top of the foot to end where you began. Do this three times, overlapping slightly.
4. Make figure eights. Start on the inside anchor, go under the arch, and behind the Achilles tendon. Wrap twice.
5. Dress the brace. Cover holes to eliminate spots where skin could abrade.

NECK

Improvise a cervical collar by rolling an insulating layer from the bottom up with sleeves out. Place under the chin, wrap sleeves around the back of the neck, and tie them with an overhand knot in the front (make sure not to obstruct airways). For more serious neck injuries, refer to neck and spine section above.

FOREARM

1. Apply padding to the forearm. Add rigidity with a stick or aluminum pack stay that extends from the elbow to at least the palm.

5 RULES FOR SPLINTING

According to NOLS Wilderness Medical Institute Curriculum Director Tod Schimelpfenig, all splints should have these characteristics:

1. Be padded.
2. Be rigid but adjustable.
3. Immobilize joints above and below the injury.
4. Be comfy.
5. Offer access to extremities so you can monitor CSM—circulation, sensation, motion—at regular intervals.

2. Secure with wide strips of fabric (bandannas, long socks, and duct tape work well). Make sure to fasten the splint below the wrist (to the hand or fingers) to immobilize the joint.
3. Finish with a sling (see the section on the upper arm). For a broken hand, extend the splint to the fingers and place balled-up socks in the hand. Buddy-tape all the fingers together to prevent accidental or reflexive movement.

LOWER LEG

1. Cut a foam pad or fold an inflatable pad so it's wide enough to wrap the leg and long enough to extend from the top of the femur to about 8 inches past the patient's foot. Slide under the leg.
2. Add padding under the knee and around the ankle. Keep it smooth to avoid hot spots.
3. Secure the pad with two or three ties (paracord, strips of cloth) above and below the knee. Close with a surgeon's knot (see Hack This: Surgeon's Knot on page 157).
4. Fold the excess padding under and tie to create an open-toed boot. Inflate pad slowly.

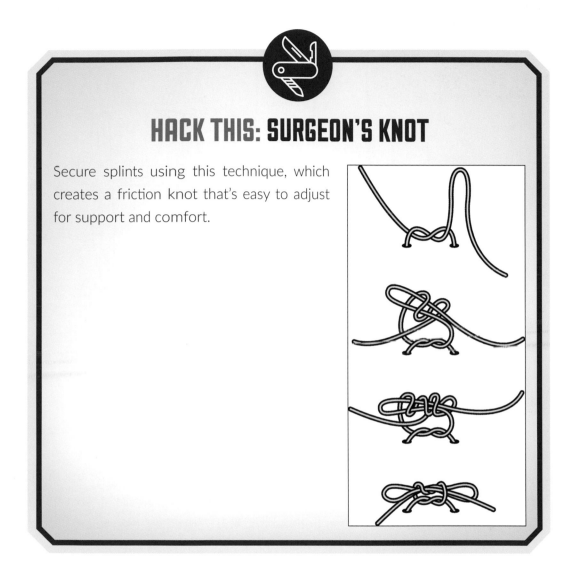

HACK THIS: SURGEON'S KNOT

Secure splints using this technique, which creates a friction knot that's easy to adjust for support and comfort.

Setting a Broken Femur

It takes a lot of force to snap the strongest bone in your body. But if you do, the damage can be severe: Jagged edges along the break can shred nerves and blood vessels, causing severe internal bleeding into the thigh and massive swelling. It's unlikely that one broken femur will kill you from blood loss—but two might. Muscle spasms can worsen the damage by yanking the bone ends until they overlap, visibly shortening the broken leg. And if the break is bad enough to force one end through the skin—an open fracture—you risk debilitating bone infection.

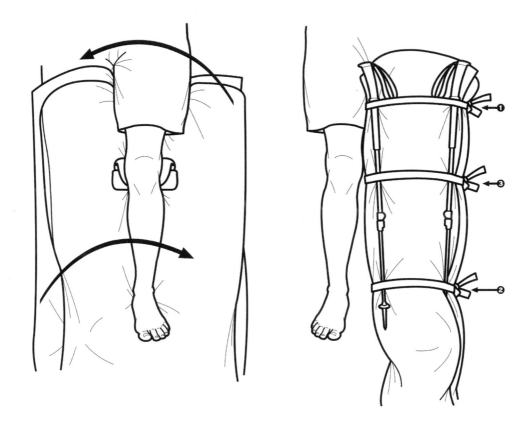

Gently pull the leg into normal, neutral alignment (pros call this in-line traction). Then immobilize it with an improvised sandwich splint: Place a sleeping bag on top of a deflated sleeping pad and wrap both around the injured leg (the splint should extend beyond the victim's foot). Put rolled socks or a hat under the person's knee to maintain a slight bend. Run two taped-together trekking poles along each side of the leg for stability; tie in place with straps or cloth strips, securing the top of the splint, then the ankle, then the center.

// WE'VE GOT A BLEEDER: TREATING GUSHING WOUNDS

First the good news: Spewing arterial bleeds usually require an explosion, gunshot, or chainsaw to truly get going. Life-threatening external bleeding is very rare. Still, if it does happen, quick action is imperative: Untreated, an arterial spurter can kill within three minutes. If your hiking partner springs a gusher after taking a fall on an iffy scramble miles from the trailhead, here's what to do.

Stop the Bleeding

Use firm hand pressure and gauze (or your cleanest T-shirt) to stanch the flow. If possible, lift the wound above heart level and hold pressure steady for at least 10 minutes. If surface pressure won't stop the bleed, you may have to insert your fingers into the wound to put direct pressure on the vein or artery. Only consider a tourniquet if you're prepared to trade the gushing limb to save the victim's life.

A couple 2-inch and 4-inch gauze pads are all you need, but if that's not enough, use extra (clean) clothing—or improvise with a bandanna or even tampons.

Clean the Cut

A dirty wound is the perfect place for a bacteria-laden infection. Prevent it: Once bleeding stops, lift the dressing and direct potable water into the wound at a perpendicular angle from 1 to 2 inches away. Use at least 8 ounces of water, or as much as needed to flush dirt and debris from inside the wound.

If there's absolutely no treated water available, you have options. If you are in a group, while one person stops the bleed, have another boil water to use for washing out the wound (let it cool before using). If you are alone, make a judgment call on clean-ish sources of water, like creeks or springs.

Pack latex gloves on every trip (in a ziplock bag). Also add a plastic syringe—the wound-spraying tool of choice for EMTs—to your first aid kit. (Improvise with your hydration-bladder hose.)

Assess Ripped Skin

Got a gaper? Leave suturing to the pros, but use ¼- to ½-inch-wide strips of medical or duct tape to close a cut (see the sidebar on closing wounds on page 160). Know

CLOSE THE WOUND

Not all wounds should be closed; especially if they are jagged, require repeated cleaning, or are even a little dirty. But an exceptionally clean and neat cut with minimal infection risk—like a slice from a knife while cooking—can be safely closed once properly cleaned and cared for.

A. After bleeding stops and the cut is cleaned, trim ¼- to ½-inch-wide strips of duct or medical tape long enough so they will extend at least 1 inch beyond each side of the gash. Starting in the middle of the wound, apply strips of tape in pairs: First, attach the end of each strip to opposite sides of the cut. Then, gently pull the strips to close the wound, and adhere the loose ends to the cut's far side.

B. Continue placing pairs of tape strips above and below the center closure (allowing ⅛ inch between strips of tape) until the wound is fully closed. Dress the cut to keep dirt out, and check it regularly for signs of infection.

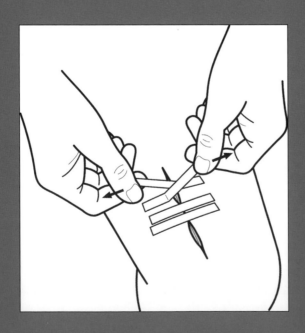

when to leave wounds open: Animal bites, crushing injuries, and punctures are all at high risk for infection. Pack with moist gauze and dress as best you can, but don't close them. Superglue is FDA-approved for skin, but save it for very neat, clean cuts (like a knife slip), because you risk sealing bacteria inside. Better? Dermabond (amazon.com) is easier to remove for follow-up care.

Keep tape and even moleskin in place by first applying Mastisol Liquid Adhesive, a medical glue that makes skin super sticky (amazon.com).

Impaled in the movies, heroes agonize over ripping out stuck arrows and spears. In real life? Leave the object in place unless it obstructs an airway, will fall out on its own, or prevents you from moving the victim.

Dress the Wound

Irrigate, then dress the wound with a moistened pad (use antibiotic ointment if you have it), followed by a dry one. Far from help? Change a wound's dressing every twelve hours, being careful not to restart bleeding when you remove padding. Monitor closely for infection. If the wound starts to swell, ooze, stink, or turn red, reopen the dressing, clean the wound, and leave it open. See signs of infection? Get to a hospital ASAP; deadly sepsis can set in within six hours.

Only have dirty clothes? Boil them. If you don't have a multiday supply of gauze, you can boil, dry, then reuse it.

Stuff a few antibiotics into your first aid kit. (Ask your family doc about a prescription for ciprofloxacin or azithromycin.) They'll slow the onset of most infections.

Prevent Shock

After you've stopped a bleed, expect and preempt shock. Symptoms include a weakening, rapid pulse; gray, cool, or clammy skin; nausea; and shallow breathing. Essentially, you'll need to maintain blood flow to a victim's brain. Lay your victim down, elevate his or her feet 6 to 10 inches, and keep the person warm and hydrated. Prepare to turn the person on his or her side to prevent choking if vomiting occurs.

// BURN NOTICE: TREATING THIRD-DEGREE BURNS

Most backcountry burns are minor; typically, it takes something as serious as prolonged contact with a campfire, falling into a Yellowstone hot spring, or getting caught in a wildfire to produce deep-tissue burns that sear the epidermis, dermis, and sometimes deeper tissues. Telltale signs of a severe burn: dry, leathery, unnaturally colored (black, brown, white, or gray) and/or charred skin. Any full-thickness burn (third- and fourth-degree burns involving both layers of skin and possibly underlying tissue) that covers more than 10 percent of the victim's body is life-threatening. (For reference: An adult arm is about 9 percent of the body, while a leg accounts for 18 percent.)

Treatment

Get the victim away from the burn source (obviously), apply cool water if the skin isn't broken, cover the burn with 2nd Skin burn pads, gauze, or clean cloth—don't attempt to remove clothing stuck to the skin—and evacuate ASAP. Give as much fluid (diluted Gatorade or a solution of a teaspoon of salt and a teaspoon of baking soda in water are best) as the victim can tolerate to prevent dehydration and shock.

// AIR SUPPORT: LUNG INJURIES

Blunt trauma to the chest usually can't do more than break a rib—painful, but not life-threatening. But in rare cases, a broken rib can stab into a lung, letting air leak into the space between the lungs and the chest wall. If the air can't escape (called a tension pneumothorax), pressure builds. First, the injured lung collapses. Then mounting pressure pushes the heart and blood vessels toward the uninjured side, compressing them until breathing and/or circulation stop.

SKIN BURN

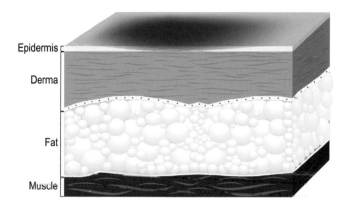

Epidermis
Derma
Fat
Muscle

First-degree burn

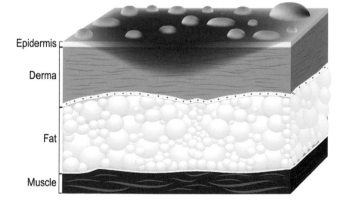

Epidermis
Derma
Fat
Muscle

Second-degree burn

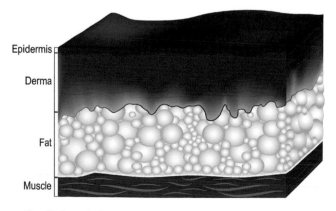

Epidermis
Derma
Fat
Muscle

Third-degree burn

➤ Credit: istockphoto

Treatment

If a victim of chest trauma experiences sharp pain, increasingly struggles to breathe, and his or her neck veins bulge, carry him or her (or slowly walk, if that's the only option) to help immediately.

// KEEP THE BEAT: TREATING HEART ATTACKS

Don't laugh: More people die in national parks from heart disease than from anything else except car wrecks. Look for chest pain that radiates to the shoulder, arm, or jaw (especially on the left side), nausea, lightheadedness, and pale, cool, sweaty skin.

> ➤ *If a chest trauma victim struggles to breathe, get help immediately.* Credit: istockphoto

Treatment

Keep the person comfortably at rest, cover him or her with clothing or a sleeping bag to prevent heat loss, and keep the person as calm as possible. Give an aspirin tablet (to inhibit artery-clogging blood clots). Don't let the person walk. Get help.

// THE AWFUL TOOTH: TREATING DENTAL INJURIES

Toothache? Rinse your mouth with a solution of half a teaspoon of salt and eight ounces of water several times a day. If pain, sensitivity to hot and cold, and swelling exist, get to a dentist—it could be an abscess. If it's a broken tooth, rinse the tooth thoroughly with drinking water, then protect the sensitive nerve by placing a chewed piece of gum over the break. Apply a cold-water bladder to the cheek to reduce swelling, and take ibuprofen for the pain. Hike out to your dentist.

// DO THE TWIST: SPRAINED AND BROKEN ANKLES

This is arguably the most common backcountry injury—all it takes is a rock shifting to fold your ankle like a flimsy tent stake. As soon as your foot begins to throb, loosen your boot but don't remove it (swelling could make it hard to put back on). Test your ankle. If it can't bear weight, you feel severe stabbing pains, and you heard a "pop" when it twisted, you have a fracture or severed ligaments. Improvise a splint (see page 155), then evacuate.

Treatment

If the pain is manageable, you're probably facing a bad sprain (stretched or partially torn ligaments). Apply a water bladder or ziplock bag filled with cool water or snow as soon as possible to limit inflammation and speed healing. After thirty minutes, wrap your foot by threading an ACE bandage under your arch and around your ankle in a figure-eight pattern. Tie your boot as tight as you can stand it, and try walking. Offload gear to lighten your backpack, and make a crutch by wrapping a T-shirt over a pole. Your routine until you reach the nearest trailhead is RICE: rest, ice (or cold water), compression, and elevation. Stop every hour to elevate and cool your ankle. Down ibuprofen to dull pain and reduce inflammation.

// ENVIRONMENTAL IMPACT: ELEMENTAL INJURIES

As much as we try to protect ourselves from extreme elements, sometimes Mother Nature wins and knocks us for a loop. Snow, altitude, wind, exposure to extreme temps: The resulting wild wounds are injuries you usually don't get back in civilization, and they often require special treatment. This is especially true in the field, where you will remain at risk until you escape.

> *Snow blindness, hypothermia, and more can result from unexpected exposure to a frozen wasteland.*
Credit: istockphoto

Snow Blindness

Redness, tearing, and a sandpapery pain when opening or moving the eye are signs of sunburned corneas. **Treatment:** Don't rub the eyes; it could further damage the corneas. Give ibuprofen for the pain, apply a cold compress, and cover the eyes with gauze. Wear sunglasses and stay in a dark environment until vision returns to normal (usually about eighteen hours).

Hypothermia

A person will often start by complaining of feeling cold, and will shiver uncontrollably. More advanced hypothermia patients exhibit "the umbles": stumbling, fumbling, mumbling, and grumbling. **Treatment:** Get the patient into warm, dry clothes and place him or her in a sheltered area—in a sleeping bag, inside of a tent. Don't have a tent? Protect the person from the elements by wrapping the sleeping bag in a tarp, plastic sheet, or garbage bags. Give water and simple sugars, such as hot chocolate or candy, to generate quick body heat. For more advanced cases, build a fire nearby and put the patient in a "hypothermia wrap." Start with a sleeping pad, put a zipped sleeping bag on top, then lay the patient (in a second sleeping bag) on that. Give the person a hot water bottle wrapped in clothing to hold in his or her hands. Put another sleeping bag on top, then wrap it all, burrito-style, in a tarp or plastic sheet.

Altitude Sickness

It starts with a hungover feeling. If you've got a headache, nausea, insomnia, lack of appetite, and fatigue—and you're above 8,000 feet—it's probably acute mountain sickness (AMS). **Treatment:** Don't go higher. Take ibuprofen for the headache, drink lots of water, and do light exercise around camp. If the symptoms don't resolve within twenty-four to forty-eight hours, descend. Head down immediately if you experience loss of coordination or persistent shortness of breath at rest; it could be a more serious altitude-related condition.

Frostbite

Cold, pale, numb, and rigid skin means that tissue has frozen. **Treatment:** Rapidly and immediately warm the area in a container of 99°F to 102°F water until the skin is pink (it takes thirty to forty-five minutes), monitoring and adding more hot water as needed to make sure the temperature is constant. Give ibuprofen for the pain. Never rub the site or expose it to high heat. If blisters form, protect them from popping. *Note:* If there's any chance of the tissue refreezing, do not warm the injury. Instead, keep it frozen until you can get the patient to a doctor.

Sunburn

You should know this one, unless you've been ultra-diligent with the sunscreen since childhood or grew up under a literal rock. Symptoms include redness, burning, lobster nicknames, perpetual embarrassment, etc. **Treatment:** Cool the skin with cold water, apply a moisturizer, take ibuprofen for pain and inflammation, drink plenty of fluids, and stay out of direct sunlight. If blisters form, consult a doctor when you return.

Heat Exhaustion

Fatigue, thirst, nausea, dizziness, and heavy sweating while out in a hot environment are signs that the body's core temperature is dangerously high. **Treatment:** Have the patient rest in the shade and drink water, a sports drink, or a diluted sugary drink (add an electrolyte tablet from your first aid kit). Spray or splash water on the patient, or place cold packs on his or her neck and groin.

Mushroom and Plant Poisoning

Treat all unknown 'shrooms as deadly—the bad ones are that bad. Induce vomiting as soon as possible after ingestion by having the patient stick a finger down his or her throat to stimulate the gag reflex. Give plenty of fluids to dilute the poison, keep a sample of the mushroom or plant, and get to a doctor. Poisoning symptoms take six to twenty-four hours to appear—and by then, it's often too late.

// WILD WOUNDS: ANIMAL BITES AND INJURIES

We might love backcountry wildlife, but love bites. Chomps and stings from critters large and small require specialized, often divergent care (a tick wound does not equal a dog wound, for example). You've likely had experience with these injuries as a child playing outside. But if that is ancient history (or you preferred video games in your youth), here's a refresher.

Bees and Wasps

If the stinger remains in the skin, remove it immediately—sometimes it's easiest to scrape a credit card along the skin to get it out. Apply a cold pack for pain and

➤ Credit: istockphoto

BUILD AN ULTRALIGHT FIRST AID KIT

Don't just rely on duct tape: All the first aid know-how in the world is useless without the right supplies to put it into action. But store-bought kits aren't always built with the trail in mind. Better option: Make an ultralight kit yourself. Start with this basic list and customize to your needs and trip requirements.

- ➤ 4 adhesive bandages
- ➤ ACE bandage
- ➤ 2 2-packs ibuprofen
- ➤ 1 roll gauze
- ➤ ½ roll medical tape
- ➤ SAM splint
- ➤ 2 knuckle adhesive bandages
- ➤ Syringe
- ➤ GlacierGel for burns/blisters
- ➤ 3 antiseptic wipes
- ➤ 4 butterfly bandages
- ➤ 2 packs antibiotic salve
- ➤ 2 packs antihistamine
- ➤ 2 packs antidiarrheal
- ➤ Tweezers
- ➤ Nitrile gloves
- ➤ 4 safety pins
- ➤ 4⅝- by 3⅜-inch sheets of moleskin
- ➤ 1.3-ounce tube of cream for sore muscles and bruising
- ➤ 2 packs powdered drink (emergency electrolytes, energy)
- ➤ 2 water treatment tabs
- ➤ Waterproof zipper bag (doubles as an irrigation syringe)
- ➤ Paper and pen/pencil

swelling, and give an oral antihistamine. If the patient has an allergic reaction—difficulty breathing, tightness of the chest, swelling of the throat, dizziness—give a dose of injectable epinephrine (prescription required) and the antihistamine. Evacuate to medical attention ASAP, keeping a second dose of epinephrine on hand and giving more antihistamine every four to six hours.

Ticks

These bloodsuckers can transmit disease if allowed to embed in the skin (sometimes a few hours is all it takes), so check yourself twice a day. If you find one, remove it immediately with tweezers. Grasp the tick at skin level, perpendicular to the long axis of the tick, and pull it gently straight out. Wash the site. If illness and/or an unusual rash develop, consult a doctor.

Venomous Spiders

Black widow bites can be tough to diagnose (many victims don't feel the bite when it occurs). Look for vomiting, weakness, headache, fever, and intense abdominal and/or back pain. Brown recluse spider bites might sting or itch. For both, clean the wound, apply cold to the site, and give the patient an antihistamine (for itching) and ibuprofen for pain. Hike out to a doctor (don't worry—death is rare).

Venomous Snakes

First, keep the victim calm (a low heart rate minimizes venom circulation, and death from snakebite is unlikely). Remove jewelry, watches, and any snug clothing that could cut off circulation when the bite site swells. Splint the bitten arm or leg, but do not elevate it. Carry the victim out if you can; otherwise, have him or her slowly walk out for a dose of antivenin.

HACK THIS: FIRST AID IMPROV

"Be prepared" is a great maxim, but we know it's unlikely you'll always have what you need in every situation. Get creative: Everyday items can serve as medical equipment in a pinch.

Antacid: Eat two teaspoons of menthol toothpaste mixed with cold water.

Antibacterial Ointment: Use honey to discourage infection and promote healing. (It's a natural antibacterial agent.) Spread it over the surface of minor cuts, burns, abrasions, and frostbite (but not directly in a wound), and cover with gauze.

Bandage: Cut a thin strip of fabric out of a T-shirt (snip in a circular pattern around the shirt to get the longest dressing possible).

Ice Pack: Soak the injury in cold water, or wrap soaked bandannas or cotton T-shirts around the site.

Irrigation Syringe: Force water out of a hydration tube or squeeze a ziplock bag with a pinhole poked in it.

Medical Gloves: Put your hands inside clean ziplock bags.

Sling: Pull the bottom of the patient's short-sleeve shirt up and over the injured arm and pin it to the front with two safety pins. Long-sleeve shirt? Pin the sleeve of the injured arm (with the arm in it) to the shirt.

Wound Closure Strips: Cut ¼-inch-long strips of duct tape; punch pinholes to let fluid drain.

Mammals

Stop any bleeding. Immediately wash the wound thoroughly with soap and water. Rinse clean, cover with a sterile dressing smeared with antibacterial ointment, and find a doctor ASAP. These bites have a high risk of infection, including rabies—and, in that case, the victim needs a vaccination within seventy-two hours, or they're toast.

> *Bandaging a patient is only the beginning. Stay alert and record reactions to keep them safe.* Credit: istockphoto

// GAME PLAN: MONITORING YOUR PATIENT

You've stabilized a serious backcountry injury or illness. You're not out of the woods yet: The next step is to prevent the patient from worsening and record symptoms and conditions for further treatment from you or first responders. Organization goes a long way—here are some key steps.

Take Notes

This is why most wilderness docs include a pencil and pad in their first aid kits. Keeping detailed notes will help you both manage ongoing treatment and safety, and offer comprehensive info when it comes time to hand the patient off to medical pros. Make a **SOAP** note—an acronym for an incident's subjective and objective elements, your assessment, and your treatment plan.

> **Subjective:** Include the patient's age, sex, and a description of the incident as the victim describes it. Include the chief complaint, spinal injury assessment, and responsiveness.

> **Objective:** Detail your evaluation. How did you find the patient? Include vital signs and pertinent negatives by taking and including SAMPLE history from the patient (Signs, Allergies, Medications, Past illnesses, Last oral intake, Events leading up to injury).

> **Assessment:** Prioritize a list of injuries and conditions that may complicate rescue and evacuation, or that may need monitoring.

> **Plan:** Outline a strategy for managing patient needs over time. Consider potential problems and environmental factors, like keeping an immobile patient warm and dry.

Measure Key Vital Signs

The condition of a seemingly stable patient can change quickly, so record vitals every five minutes. After three rounds of stable results, double the time between monitoring. Here's how to gauge two tricky vitals that can indicate worsening conditions.

> **Level of responsiveness (LOR):** This changes quickly and indicates possible brain injuries and the severity of other conditions. If the patient is alert, ask him or her four questions: What's your name? Where are you? What day is it? What happened? Fewer than three correct answers is abnormal. Patient not alert (that is, unable to answer)? A verbally responsive patient reacts to loud noises. A pain-responsive one winces or groans when you pinch him. If a victim is not alert, maintain the airway, check for breathing and circulation, and manage life threats while looking for LOR improvements.

➤ **Blood pressure:** No radial (wrist) pulse or one that's weakening could indicate dropping blood pressure and a seriously worsening patient. In the backcountry, alertness, a strong radial pulse, and normal skin color/temperature/moisture together indicate adequate blood pressure. If you suspect blood pressure is dropping, look for and treat the possible cause.

HACK THIS: NATURAL MEDICINES

Finding wild medicines usually requires a lifetime of training (there's a reason shamans are old). But these three easily identifiable plants are found widely across North America and offer natural relief.

- **Arnica Gel:** A sunflower relative found in Western states, arnica's flowers and roots contain glycosides, which have anti-inflammatory and anti-swelling properties. Grind both into a paste, and apply this to sprains, bruises, and strained muscles immediately after an injury to relieve pain. Don't put it on open wounds or take it orally.

- **Yarrow:** Known as the nosebleed plant, this white-flowering herb contains an alkaloid that can accelerate clotting. Steep yarrow in hot water for five minutes, and use the tea to wash a cut or scrape. You can also apply dried herbs directly to a wound.

- **Old-Man's Beard:** People have applied old-man's beard (*usnea*) as an antiseptic for centuries. These greenish, hairlike tufts of hanging lichens grow on tree branches worldwide (it looks a bit like Spanish moss). Pull back the main stem's sheath; *usnea* has a white cord in the center. Place a clump on the cut.

Ice is everywhere in the winter wild—and it can do you some good. Put this common material to work in a survival situation with these six techniques.

MAKE FIRE

Use a rock to harvest a clear palm-size piece of ice—lake ice at least a few feet from the shore is a good bet. Use the heat from your bare hands to shape it into an inch-thick lens that's convex (bulging out) on both sides. Then, holding your ice lens with gloved hands, use it like a magnifying glass to concentrate the sun. (**Note:** If you think you may someday use this—or just want to impress your friends—practice like crazy. Everything about this technique is hard.)

SIGNAL FOR HELP

Ice can make a decent reflector if properly shaped into a convex geometry that concentrates light. Shape clear ice (as above) and practice shining your lens on a nearby surface to get a sense for how it works. Use this to signal aircraft. Need dispersed light instead? Put your headlamp against a chunk of cloudy ice.

FIX BROKEN GEAR

In subzero conditions, Canadian survival instructors have long used ice as a makeshift glue by wetting moss, lichen, or cloth, wrapping the patch of vegetation or cloth around objects such as broken tent poles, and waiting for the bandage to freeze into place.

ADD STICKING POWER

Make your tent stakes or deadman anchors stronger in snow by dumping a cup or two of water (sourced from a creek or bottle) on them and letting it freeze.

TREAT INJURIES

Ice reduces swelling and pain, and can even help slow blood flow from an injury. Apply ice in twenty-minute increments, and check the wound to ensure it's not getting waxy or white with cold. Keep pressure on bleeders until the flow stops.

STAY AWAKE

If there's a situation where you must stay awake, such as after suffering a concussion, tie a piece of ice to the top of your tent so it drips on your forehead. They don't call it water torture for nothing.

> ➤ Credit: istockphoto

// STAY OR GO?: EVACUATION OR RESCUE?

If your hiking buddy pitches off a cliff and sustains a severe injury, you're going to face a tough question once you've stabilized him or her: Should you go for help—or haul your buddy out? That depends on several factors, but answering a few key questions can help you make the best decision.

1. **How bad is it?** Patients with life-threatening injuries should usually stay put and wait for trained medical professionals; those with less serious injuries can walk or be carried out. If the patient can handle it, walking out is the best option.

2. **How far is the trailhead?** One fit hiker can move a lot faster than a group carrying a litter (stretcher). If you're deep in the wilderness, a messenger might bring back professional help before you can carry the patient out.

3. **Can the potential rescuer(s) handle it?** You'll need strength, stamina, and skill to navigate the terrain with an injured person in tow.

4. **What's the weather like?** Stay put if severe weather puts the rescuers in danger of getting lost or injuring themselves.

5. **Is there imminent danger?** Even severely injured patients might need to be moved if the current location is unsafe—for example, if lightning is striking or you're on an unstable slope.

Carry On: Three Rescue Methods

If you've decided to evacuate, first stabilize the patient and make sure he or she is warm, comfortable, and hydrated. Then get out as efficiently as possible. Each of the following techniques for moving a patient out of the backcountry has strengths and weaknesses, depending on the conditions of the rescuer and victim.

➤ *Sometimes evacuation requires a helping hand.* Credit: istockphoto

BACKPACK CARRY

If you are one rescuer carrying a smaller, lighter patient, start by unzipping the sleeping bag compartment on a pack. Have the patient get in the pack by sticking his or her legs through the unzipped compartment, cutting holes to fit if necessary (you can also cut leg holes in a pack with no sleeping bag compartment). The rescuer then shoulders the pack with the patient in it.

TWO-PERSON POLE CARRY

Two rescuers moving over relatively easy terrain can tape or bind two ski poles, trekking poles, or sturdy branches together and attach them to the bottoms of the rescuers' backpacks using their ice axe loops, compression straps, and extra webbing (you can also slide the poles between the rescuers' backs and their packs, on top of the hip belts). Place a folded sleeping pad or extra clothing on the poles to make a seat. Have the patient sit on it with his or her arms over the shoulders of each rescuer.

STRETCHER

Groups of at least six (at least four to carry the litter, two to clear and scout the trail) can attempt to build an improvised stretcher to cover short distances. Turn the sleeves of two (or more) jackets or T-shirts inside out, zip them up, and lay them on the ground, hem to hem. Slide two sturdy branches or skis through the sleeves (they should be about 2 feet longer than the patient). Place the patient on the jackets and have rescuers grab the branches and lift.

PARALYZED

BY CAMERON ZICK AS
TOLD TO EMELIE FROJEN

// WE LEFT FOR THE SUMMIT OF MOUNT SNEFFELS, A COLORADO FOURTEENER, AT 9 A.M., STARTING OUR SPRING CLIMB EARLY TO AVOID AN EVENING SNOWSTORM IN THE FORECAST.

There were six of us, all friends from college, on a reunion four years after graduation. We started up the trail amid spring flowers and vibrant green trees, but soon they gave way to waist-deep snow etched with little rivulets of snowmelt.

Two miles of deep, crusty snow delivered us to a talus field. Half of the group, myself included,

came underdressed for snow, and so, less than halfway to the summit, we all decided to side with safety and descend. No matter. We'd come out here for fun and camaraderie.

On the hike back down, we passed a 5-foot-tall boulder with a great view of Sneffels and the Uncompahgre National Forest. We all scrambled to the top and set up the camera tripod—if we

> ## "BY SHUTTING MY EYES, MY MIND COULD DISCONNECT FROM THE TERRIFYING SIGHT OF MY PARALYZED BODY."

Paralyzed and Powerless

The second I landed in the snowbank, I knew something was wrong. My head was submerged in the snow, my body straight up in the air, like a light post driven into concrete. I couldn't move my arms or legs.

I screamed for help, but when I opened my mouth I swallowed snow, suffocating me. For a moment, I stopped to listen for help coming, but all I heard was laughter from my friends.

What if no one comes to help? The idea sucked at my energy and my air. But then I reminded myself, *I'm twenty-five years old; there's no way my life is ending in a 3-foot pile of snow.* I gathered a breath and stopped struggling, hoping my friends would realize I was in trouble. The laughter stopped.

I felt my head move out of the snow and into the light as Michael lifted me by my ankles. I immediately told my friends that I'd lost all movement below the neck and to be very careful. From my awkward upside-down angle, I looked around at the group, all of whom stood in stunned silence.

Immediately, two of my friends, Drew and Ben, took off down the mountain in search of

couldn't make the summit, we at least would get our hero shot.

As we downclimbed, Michael jumped off the rock into a pile of fluffy snow, landing on his side. It looked like fun. This whole hike I'd erred on the conservative side, since I was dressed in shorts, but now felt like the right time to soak up the snow. I figured I'd warm up on the hike down.

I planned out my moves and scrambled down to a spot on the rock that looked like it had a good angle to dismount from the boulder. But as I maneuvered, my foot slipped on a bit of ice and sent me falling headfirst.

➤ Credit: Bob Stefko

help. Michael, Sean, and Spencer stayed with me. Michael slowly lowered me down flat onto the snow that just moments before had trapped me. He then lay behind me and rested my back and neck on his stomach, figuring it was the most flat and comfortable way to hold my spine in alignment.

Hypothermia Threatens

As the evening progressed the forecasted storm rolled in, with flying snow and falling temperatures. Snow accumulated on my limp body but I felt no sensation from anywhere but my face. Michael, still lying on the snow cradling me, started to get very cold.

By this time, I was later told, Drew and Ben had reached the bottom of the trail. They ran into a stranger who gave them her phone, and they called for help.

Back on the mountain, Sean and Spencer spotted a lone pine in a talus field that seemed large enough to shelter us from the snow. Michael and Spencer were always the prepared ones on our outings. On this day hike, they'd brought survival tools and overnight camping supplies. We began brainstorming how to get me under the tree. The planning kept my mind off my injury.

Spencer pulled an inflatable sleeping pad from his pack and blew it up. The group delicately stabilized my neck, rolled me onto my side, and slid the pad under me. Then, they finally got cell reception and called our friend Josh, a neurosurgeon. By luck and fate, he picked up and instructed my friends on how to move and care for someone with a neck injury.

While my friends were talking to Josh, I began to panic. I felt claustrophobic in my own body. Snow accumulated on my face and I couldn't move my arm to dust it off. My torso felt weightless, as if detached from my body. I calmed myself by closing my eyes and drifting into silence. By shutting my eyes, my mind could disconnect from the terrifying sight of my paralyzed body.

> **"AS BEST I COULD, I FORCED MY MIND TO THINK OF PEOPLE, PLACES, AND EXPERIENCES THAT I WANTED TO SEE AND RELIVE AGAIN."**

My friends returned and told me their plan to move me. Evenly and slowly, they lifted the sleeping pad with me on it off of the ground and walked toward the tree. There, Spencer covered me in a space blanket and my friends took shifts keeping me warm. Each person removed his extra layers and put them on me, while two friends curled up next to me to share body heat. Then they'd switch.

Waiting Game

Under the tree, all we could do was wait for the rescue team. My thoughts began to get dark and heavy. Panic and resignation came by turns: Am I paralyzed for life? Is a rescue team coming? Will I die on this mountain? When the weight of these questions overwhelmed my silence, I shouted them and obscenities into the night. I screamed because it was one of the few things my body could do.

My friends took turns calming me down. I tried to focus my mind on recovery and the things I should look forward to once I could move again, but the calm was short-lived. I stared at my arms and legs, begging them to move, but nothing would. This sequence continued for five hours—until the rescue team arrived.

But there would be no immediate salvation: The rescue crew said that a helicopter couldn't land on the mountain because of the storm. I'd have to be carried.

A team of ten packaged me up in an insulated body bag for the five-hour trek down the mountain. The inflated body bag pressed against my entire body, and, except for a hole around my face, I was locked in.

Alone with my thoughts, I found the stop-and-go hike down to be a psychological roller coaster. How painful would it be if I were dropped down the side of the mountain? What if we got lost or my body gave out before the hospital? Even if I made it to surgery, what was there to live for if I were paralyzed? I spent the majority of my time fighting this last question, and wishing I was at the hospital.

As best I could, I forced my mind to think of people, places, and experiences that I wanted to see and relive again. I pictured myself on an open field, playing baseball with my five-year-old sister. The thought of spending just one more minute with her and many of my friends and family gave me motivation to persevere.

At 1 a.m., we reached the trailhead and a waiting ambulance. It was a two-and-a-half-hour drive to St. Mary's Medical Center in Grand Junction, Colorado. But before I knew it, I was in an operating room, drifting into an anesthetic daze in advance of a twelve-hour surgery. I shut my eyes, and for the first time since the accident, my mind was quiet.

The Long Road to Recovery

I woke up in a hospital bed. Here, finally, I felt in control, able to influence the pace of my recovery. I thought back to the mountain, to the point where I almost gave up, and was glad I didn't.

I exerted every inch of effort in my body and lifted my left index finger half an inch off the bed. There was a lot of work ahead. But hour by hour and day by day, I found the strength, seizing control back from my accident and channeling it into physical therapy.

Six months after the fall, I was back on my feet. It might take months or years, but I told my friends we'll all be standing together on Mount Sneffels again soon. And we will.

THREATS | 7

What fuels wilderness nightmares? Anxious backcountry travelers don't lose sleep over the possibility of common risks like a sprained ankle. No, there are more exciting dragons to worry about: an avalanche hiding under a blanket of untouched snow; lightning on a formerly bluebird day; a bear waiting around the green bend to rearrange the food chain in real time. Knowledge and planning can't forestall every disaster; you can do everything right and still run into a dragon. But here's the thing about dragons: With luck and knowledge, you can slay them—or avoid them entirely.

In the finger-numbing morning shadow of Maine's highest peak, we started up the Pamola cliffs, a slab of fractured, lichen-covered granite rising for several hundred feet to Mount Katahdin's famous Knife Edge ridge. Below us, Chimney Pond glinted in the bright, clear-sky light. The five of us, all around thirty years old, joked and laughed in anticipation of a fun day on an easy rock climb.

We climbed as two rope teams, with one friend, Bill, and me leading. Belaying and chattering below us were my girlfriend, Penny; my longtime friend Rick, with whom I started climbing four years earlier; and Rick's girlfriend, Diane. We were on a route recommended by a ranger because another party was on the route we had intended to climb, and we didn't want to risk them accidentally knocking stones down on us. On the second pitch, 150 feet above our companions, Bill and I tried to build belay anchors. But every time I attempted to place gear in a crack, the rock around it broke off.

"Bill, how's that rock just above you?" I asked.

Bill reached up and tapped the cliff as if knocking lightly on a door, a routine test to see whether it sounded solid or hollow. With an incongruously soft scraping sound, a block of granite bigger than a large suitcase slid past him.

We both yelled, "Rock! Rock! Rock!"

The block smashed apart into a cloudburst of stone, plummeting toward our friends. I thought it would kill them all. The three flattened themselves against the cliff, trying to shrink as the rain of granite washed over them.

Then it had passed. Penny and Diane looked up, miraculously unscathed, giving me hope that Rick, who'd been struck by a piece of the rock, would be fine, too. In the brief ensuing silence, I watched him for movement, sure I would hear his steady voice announcing he was OK. But it was Penny's voice I heard, shouting upward, "Blood is gushing from his head!"

Rick hung upside down on his rope, motionless. Our attempts to resuscitate him—pumping his chest and breathing into his mouth—proved futile.

The outdoors changed for me that day, and it has never been the same since. I've replayed the events leading up to Rick's death a thousand times in my mind, looking for black-and-white evidence of where we went wrong. There isn't any.

Mountains crumble. Loose rock on a cliff is like the sudden thunderstorm hitting a peak or the rattler you didn't see. We accept these hazards when we venture outdoors.

And so I'm left with a hard lesson: It's impossible to eliminate all risk in the outdoors. Rocks slide. Trees fall. Bears behave unpredictably. Rare? Extremely. But don't fool yourself into believing that the odds could never catch up with you. The wilderness is not a theme park—nothing is a certainty, which is precisely why we go there in the first place.

Almost twenty years have somehow trickled past since Rick died. I've made my share of preventable mistakes and learned from them. I've witnessed accidents no one could predict. And still, I climb, backcountry ski, and hike through wilderness, often with my kids. Our adventures in the wild are some of the happiest times we share. But I don't pretend that the world is perfectly safe, whether in the wilderness or the frontcountry. Cars skid on icy roads. Cancer strikes. Rocks break loose.

That's why I told my kids about what happened to Rick. Not long ago, sitting at a campsite in the mountains, as the first stars emerged, I told them a story about death, but mostly, truths about life. —Michael Lanza

// ANIMAL KINGDOM: AVOIDING ATTACKS

When playing in a wilderness full of animal life, you can go far by remembering it's their world—we're just visiting. Paying attention to your surroundings and giving critters a wide berth usually prevents most incidents. Usually.

When wild animal encounters go bad, you can almost always blame hunger. Some critters want to make a meal of you; others fear it's you who wants to eat them. Here are the locations on the body where animal attacks most often occur, and how you can protect yourself when wildlife encounters get a little too close. (Statistics are averages culled from a variety of reliable sources.)

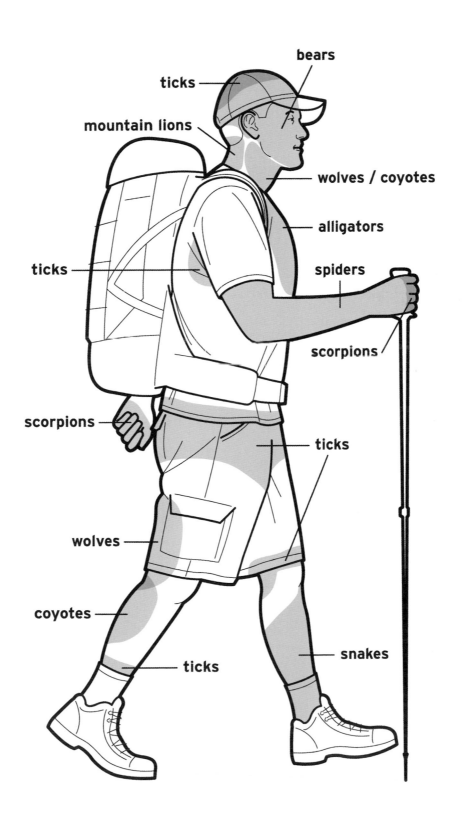

ALLIGATORS

- Targets: Chest
- Attacks: 7 per year
- Deaths: 6 (since 2008)

Big gators grab as much meat as they can, but let go about two-thirds of the time. If one bites you, don't just struggle—gouge its eyes.

BEARS

- Targets: Scalp, face
- Attacks: Unknown
- Deaths: 12 (grizzly); 10 (black) (since 2003)

If a grizzly gets you to the ground, roll onto your stomach, play dead, and protect your head. If it's a black bear, fight like mad. (No, we're not done with bears yet—see more below.)

COYOTES

- Targets: Calves, throat
- Attacks: 5
- Deaths: 1 (since 2008)

Coyotes go for the legs to down their prey, then they use their jaws to crush the windpipe. Stay upright and balanced by jabbing them with a stick or trekking pole.

MOUNTAIN LIONS

- Targets: Back of neck
- Attacks: 6 per year (average)
- Deaths: 1 (since 2008)

If stalked, make yourself look threatening, and throw rocks. If a puma clamps onto your neck, counterattack its nose, eyes, and neck.

SCORPIONS

> ➤ Targets: Fingers
> ➤ Stings: 19,131 (since 2011)
> ➤ Deaths: 4 (since 2007)

Credit a good antivenin with low fatalities. Scorpions are most active when nighttime temps top 77°F. Shake out your gear.

SNAKES

> ➤ Targets: Lower leg
> ➤ Bites: 3,137 (since 2011)
> ➤ Deaths: 22 (since 2008)

All snakebites are defensive. Avoid stepping into places you can't see. If bit, stay calm, keep the bitten limb below the heart, and evacuate.

SPIDERS

> ➤ Targets: Arms, legs
> ➤ Attacks: 3,912 (since 2011)
> ➤ Deaths: 7 per year (on average)

Black widow, brown recluse, and hobo: Most bites are defensive, but if one happens, put cold compresses on the wound and evacuate.

TICKS

> ➤ Targets: Ankles, knees, groin, armpits, head
> ➤ Bites: 1,571 (since 2011)
> ➤ Deaths: 25 (Lyme disease)

Check for ticks after each hike: Full-grown deer ticks are as tiny as pepper flakes.

WOLVES

> ➤ Targets: Legs (upper and lower), throat
> ➤ Attacks: 12 (since 2008)
> ➤ Deaths: 1 (since 2008)

Wolf bites are extremely rare, but if one attacks, shove your fist down its throat so the animal can't breathe.

// BEAR NECESSITIES: STAY SAFE IN YOGI'S HOUSE

If wild places have a Big Bad, you can bet it's a bear. It makes sense. They weigh hundreds of pounds, can rip apart cars with their bare claws, and, yes, can kill you with the same. The fact that attacks are exceedingly rare and that most bears want almost nothing to do with us does little to dull the prickly fear they instill in us. But science can: Understanding how bears behave, what to expect, and how best to manage your behavior in their presence imparts loads of bear country confidence. You'll both feel safer and increase the likelihood that, should you be lucky enough to see a bruin, the only thing you'll experience is awe.

Know Your Average Bear

First, it's worthwhile to understand the differences in the two species of bear you are likely to encounter in the wild (unless you are a polar explorer). Recognizing their distinct but overlapping characteristics and behaviors can make all the difference in an encounter.

GRIZZLY/BROWN BEARS

The terrifying giants that spooked Lewis and Clark in the Great Plains used to range from Kansas to California—but now they mostly live in Wyoming, Montana, Idaho, western Canada, and Alaska (where they usually call them brown bears). Washington has a very small population. They can live in dense forests, arctic tundra, and even

> ➤ *This is a grizzly. Don't get this close.* Credit: istockphoto

on open plains, but they prefer alpine meadows. Grizzlies can grow as tall as 8 feet and weigh up to 800 pounds (some large browns on Kodiak and Admiralty Islands in Alaska can top 10 feet and 1,500 pounds). They are usually brown, but can have white-tipped or "grizzled" fur. Cubs and subadults can climb trees, but they rarely do so as adults. In pursuit of the winter blubber that keeps them alive through nine months of hibernation, they eat a highly adaptable diet that ranges from salmon to berries to moths to grass to caribou calves. In most ecosystems, plants make up the majority of their diet—sometimes as much as 90 percent. They are highly territorial and aggressive, especially mothers with cubs, and despite their bulk a sprinting grizzly can outrun Usain Bolt at 30-plus miles per hour. While they surely can eat people, attacks are more likely attempts to neutralize perceived threats.

BLACK BEARS

Black bears are far more common than grizzlies throughout North America, with significant populations in most states (even New Jersey). They prefer dense forests, but are even more adaptable than grizzlies, and can be found almost everywhere— swamps, deserts, alpine zones, and even Walmart parking lots. The name "black bear" is a bit misleading: They can be jet black, silvery blue, blue-black, brown, cinnamon, blonde, and everything in between—the rare Kermode subspecies in British Columbia is even white. Much smaller than grizzlies, they usually stretch 5 to 6 feet long and weigh 200 to 600 pounds. Speedy blacks can reach speeds of 35 miles per hour, and remain expert tree climbers into adulthood. Compared to their aggressive cousins, black bears are shy and more prone to running away; mothers with cubs are more likely to climb trees than mount an attack. Most "attacks" are bites or claw swipes that happen when people get too close or corner them. Nevertheless, they are formidable, ultra-strong predators capable of killing and eating humans. Rule of thumb: If a black bear attacks, it's trying to eat you.

Both grizzlies and blacks have moderate eyesight (poor vision is a myth) and hearing that is more than twice as strong as ours. But it's all about the nose: A bear's sense of smell is seven times stronger than a bloodhound's and *2,100 times* stronger than ours.

Bear Safety Everyone Should Know

Now that you are familiar with our bear brethren, you can concentrate on safety. Here are some key skills every hiker should know before entering bear country.

PREVENT AN ENCOUNTER
Here are some easy things to do to prevent bear encounters.
1. **Don't hike alone.** Bears are less likely to attack groups than individuals.
2. **Make noise.** For real: Bells don't always work and are annoying, so stick to moderately noisy conversation to better alert bears to your presence. Aim for conversation-at-a-bar volume—you don't have to shout unless you are

> *Making regular noise can ensure you never have to see a grizzly in charge posture or close enough to count its hairs.* Credit: istockphoto

near loud rivers or wind noise picks up. Singing is even better, especially if you're alone ("Running with the Devil" is my go-to). Given the opportunity, most bears will avoid a human encounter if they can detect you first.

3. **Carry bear spray.** Keep it handy (a charging bear won't wait for you to dig it out of your pack). Know how to use it. Pay attention to weather conditions: Wind and rain can mess with accuracy and potency.

4. **Be scent smart.** Store food in bear canisters or hang it properly. Avoid fragrance-heavy shampoos and hygiene products; they smell just like food, so put them in your canister or bear bag. Cook in a separate area away from your tent. Don't leave any smelly items in your tent, and change clothes after you cook. Bear spray isn't like bug spray: Never, ever preemptively fire bear spray around your tent. It's made from peppers; it's like marinating your campsite.

5. **Stay vigilant.** Paying attention to terrain features can give you an advantage. If you come to a section of trail with recent evidence of bears (such as scat or overturned stumps), make extra noise. Give bears a chance to hear you and flee before their protective instincts kick in.

Dealing with Close Encounters

Bears are wild animals, which means they're unpredictable. If you take every precaution but still have a run-in, here's how you deal with bears in close encounters.

1. **Leave the area.** If you spot a bear at distance, make a wide detour to leave the area calmly as soon as possible. Anything closer than 200 yards is too close.

2. **Don't panic.** In a low voice, announce your presence and back away slowly. Don't run: Flight will trigger a bear's prey drive, and they are faster than you are. If the bear stands up, don't freak out—it's just checking you out. If the bear huffs, snaps its jaws, or growls at you—his way of expressing aggression—speak louder but continue moving away slowly.

3. **Stand your ground in a charge.** Most bear charges are bluffs. If you have bear spray (you should, and it should be within reach) and the bear is approaching within 20 yards, spray a low cloud that envelops the charging bruin. Get upwind of the bear if you can, but bear spray leaves the can at around 70 miles per hour (mph), so the spray remains effective at close range.

4. **Get aggressive.** If the bear approaches within 10 yards, aim slightly above its head to direct short bursts of spray into his eyes, mouth, and nose. Now's a good time for that war cry, too.

If Attacked by a Grizzly

This is maybe number one on the camper fear list. But you can face down the biggest fear, and win.

1. **Go submissive/defensive.** Is it still coming? Time to convince it you're not a threat. Lie face down with your pack on, spread your legs (making it difficult to roll you and get to vital organs), and protect your neck and head with your hands. The bear may bite you, it may just sniff you, but in most cases it will move on. Remain still while waiting for the bear to leave the area—it may return if it notices renewed movement.

2. **Climb a tree.** This is risky: Grizzlies are poor climbers, but they can ascend trees if the limbs are arranged like ladder rungs. Make sure you can climb higher than 15 feet on slender branches.

3. **Fight.** If a grizzly starts to feed on you, you have to fight. Go for the nose, eyes, and ears. Give it your all—you will either end up dead or with the best story at every party you ever go to.

If Attacked by a Black Bear

1. If a black bear maintains a sustained attack (not just a defensive swipe while fleeing the scene), it's highly likely the attack is predatory. Climbing a tree may well be useless against the notoriously arboreal black bear, and defensive submission makes its job easier. You are food: Fight, fight, fight (see above for how) and earn that story-for-life, hero.

HACK THIS: HANG A BEAR BAG IN FIVE MINUTES

Bear canisters are foolproof in any environment and are reliable, but they're bulky, expensive, heavy, and, of course, cost money. With common gear items, practice, and a couple of trees, this method works before you can even close a canister.

1. Find two trees about 20 feet apart, each with a branch at least 15 feet high.
2. Tie one end of a 100-foot, 3-millimeter utility cord (widely available at outdoor stores) to a carabiner. Tie the other around one tree's trunk.
3. Throw the rope over the first branch; pull out most of the slack, then throw it over the second tree's branch.
4. Tie a loop in the cord at least 6 feet from the nearest tree, and clip the food bag to it.
5. Pull on the free end of the cord to hoist the bag.
6. Tie off the cord to the second tree's trunk.

// DEATH FROM ABOVE ... AND EVERYWHERE ELSE

Nature is a volatile place. The ordinary processes that help make it beautiful on a macro timescale—geological, climatic—can prove deadly in their micro expressions. Wildfire, avalanches, flash floods, and lightning inspire a terror so primal we needed gods to explain them. Science didn't make it much better: These are some of the most destructive forces on earth, with fearsome statistics (speed, acreage destroyed, Boy Scouts killed) we can now measure precisely. Here's how to escape their wrath.

➤ *The average avalanche moves at 80 miles per hour.* Credit: istockphoto

Avalanche Avoidance

Avalanches rip down mountainsides at 80-plus miles per hour, and kill an average of twenty-five people a year (not just skiers; snowshoers are at high risk, too). Anyone seriously interested in winter adventure should take an avalanche safety course.

But here are a few cheats: The most destructive slides form on pitches angled between 30 and 45 degrees. Measure slope with an inclinometer or estimate it using ski poles: (1) With two poles that are equal lengths, stand one vertically on the snow (don't drive it in) and use the other pole to form an inverted L. (2) Lower the level pole straight down until the end is touching the snow. (3) If the level pole crosses halfway or above on the vertical pole, you're in the avalanche zone.

But let's say you get caught in the slide: You'll have to "swim" to safety. Assume the whitewater position: feet downhill and in a sitting position to absorb shocks of obstacles. Ditch poles, ice axes, or skis, and use your hands and arms in a swimming motion to move toward the surface and stay there.

An avalanche looks powdery, but if the blunt force trauma doesn't kill you, suffocation will. Once an avalanche stops, it hardens like concrete and forces its way down your air passages. Prep an air pocket: When the avalanche slows down, get your palms up by your forehead, elbows out,

DON'T MESS WITH A MOOSE

In Alaska, moose are responsible for more injuries than grizzly bears (up to twenty-five injuries annually in North America). Snorting, stomping, and pinned-back ears are clear signs you've wandered too close to one of these 1,000-pound behemoths. In spring and early summer, female moose will aggressively defend their calves, so stay back at least 100 yards. Male moose become belligerent during the fall rut, when they're establishing dominance. Your escape plan: Most moose charges are bluffs, but you don't want to wait around to find out if it's serious. Run away as fast as you can, keeping at least one tree between you and the moose as a buffer. Be prepared to climb at least 12 feet up a tree if the beast pursues.

> ➤ **Hoof It:** The same escape rules apply to elk and bison, and don't get any closer than 25 yards. Both of these grass munchers can be surprisingly aggressive, especially during a rut.

and start creating a cocoon around your face. Take a deep breath and hold it—the more your lungs can expand, the better. When the avalanche stops, you'll have more space to breathe in the pocket you created. Space is time, and time increases the odds of rescuers finding you before it's too late.

Outrun a Wildfire

Climate change will not be kind to us. In the past decade, wildfires in the United States have increased dramatically to 60,000 each year, burning an average total of 7.2 million acres and killing an average of thirty-five people. Fires move with dominant winds, and can attain speeds over 50 mph. But even without assistance, they can spread at 14 mph—about the top running speed of the average person.

During daylight hours, rising warm air pulls blazes upslope in a candling effect. At night, cooler air forces it back down. If you're on a hill, hightail it down. Flames lick upward and can climb slopes faster than you can. Keep an eye on the fuel around you. Grasses and dry pine needles will burn up quickest, whereas leafy greens and downed trees take longer. Bodies of water, low areas, swamps, sandy beaches, and treeless gravel washes offer the safest cover. Avoid grasslands and meadows.

Head upwind—fast—if possible, but if you're cut off, aim for a rocky, non-vegetated area. Cover your face with wet wool or cotton to filter out some smoke, and stay low to the ground. If the fire's coming and things are starting to heat up fast, hold your breath. That first gasp of superheated air kills more people than smoke inhalation does. A surrounded firefighter might put up a heat-reflecting shelter and dig a small hole in the dirt to breathe through, but without the proper equipment, stick to your first, best plan: run like hell.

Rockfall

Rockfall is a surprisingly common cause of backcountry injury and death. Human-triggered slides can occur at any time, the result of an errant step that loosens already unstable stone. Avoid hiking in the "fall line" directly beneath other hikers—spread

> ➤ *If there's a threat of lightning overnight, strongly consider where you shelter.* Credit: istockphoto

out laterally, and give space so you can dodge. Natural slides are most common in early spring, when melting ice releases hunks of rock.

If rocks start tumbling, stay on your feet and run laterally out of the fall line while protecting your head, or dash behind the nearest large boulder. Shout "Rock!" as soon as possible to alert everyone around you. If you're on a narrow ledge with nowhere to hide, take a wide stance for balance and glance upward so that you can dodge the most dangerous projectiles.

Lightning

The hand of Zeus is terrifying for good reason: Lightning can strike ground more than 25 miles from storm clouds, so blue sky overhead doesn't mean you're safe. In fact, there's no place in the backcountry that is completely safe in an electrical

5 RULES FOR CROSSING GLACIERS

Ice country is beautiful, but deadly. Watch for these five hazards to skip touching the void.

1. **Crevasses.** These fissures are mesmerizing to behold, deadly to fall into. In spring and early summer, they're often concealed by snow bridges. As the weather warms, the bridges melt, eventually exposing the crevasses. In between, crevasses can be exceptionally dangerous—hidden from view by a layer of snow too thin to hold a hiker's weight. (Caution: You can fall into one anytime, regardless of the season.) If possible, travel on a rope team of three or more.
2. **Moraines.** You can hike atop this glacial feature—an accumulation of debris like rocks and dirt—to skirt crevasse danger. But the transition from moraine to glacier can be hazardous. First, the slope tends to be steep—often as steep as possible before the slope releases—and littered with loose rocks. Second, you might encounter a "moat" between the moraine and glacier, where the ice pulls away from the rocks and leaves a dangerous gap.
3. **Moulins.** Think of these sinkholes as part of a glacier's plumbing system, transporting meltwater from the surface down into the glacier's underbelly. But on the surface, flowing water means slick glacial ice. Slip here, and you can easily be pulled into the moulin by the water's force. Avoid running water and wet ice—and wear crampons.
4. **Rockfall.** Random large boulders spread over the glacier indicate a path where rockfall is a hazard. Avoid areas with rockfall, especially in warmer weather, when rocks tend to fall. Wear a helmet.
5. **Weather.** Clear, high-pressure systems are a best bet for glacier travel. But whiteouts can descend quickly in the mountains; you should be skilled enough to navigate safely in low or no visibility.

storm, but your first move should be to seek safer terrain. Move off peaks and ridges to the lowest ground nearby. In rolling landscapes, drop into a depression, like a dry ravine. Stay away from water and isolated tall trees or towers.

If the time between the flash and the bang is less than thirty seconds (five seconds = 1 mile), consider yourself at serious risk. If you hear buzzing, or static is making your hair stand up, a strike is imminent. Assume the lightning position: Spread out, with at least 50 feet between you and other people, so that multiple people won't be struck by one bolt, thereby incapacitating a whole group. Crouch or sit with your feet close together on a foam pad or pack (without a metal frame). Standing, laying down, and having your feet wide all increase the potential damage from a direct hit. Removing metal jewelry will reduce the risk of a secondary burn, but not a lightning strike.

If there's a threat of lightning overnight, try to use the safe terrain considerations above to choose your campsite (stay off high ground, look for protected depressions). No guarantees, though: Tents offer no protection from lightning, and their metal poles may even attract it.

// WATERY GRAVE: FLASH FLOODS

Half an inch. That's all the rain it takes to trigger a deadly wall of water in the Southwest's slot canyons, where bone-dry, narrow terrain funnels deluges as deep as 15 feet in a matter of minutes. Gushing waters running more than 30 mph kill fifty people a year. Drowning is the biggest risk, but so is bodily trauma of all kinds: Flash floods hoover up debris and turn into a churning stew of sticks, sand, and rocks hurtling at you with the force of a school bus. Many are strong enough to sweep up boulders into their deadly grind.

Flood Insurance

Flash floods are most prevalent in late summer, when afternoon thunderstorms fueled by Southwest monsoons are common and the soil is dehydrated. Avoid

> *Flash floods are common and should not be crossed.* Credit: istockphoto

canyons if rain threatens, and never attempt to cross a flooded area. Watch for thunderclouds building on the horizon and get out of the canyon if they appear. Know the signs of an impending flash flood—a sudden increase in water depth or speed, water turning muddy or dark, floating debris, and a jet engine–like roar—and get to high ground immediately if you detect them.

If you're caught, you're in for it. Check canyon walls for bundles of sticks and other debris that indicate previous flood levels. You need to hike or climb above that high-water mark if a flood surprises you. No luck? Seek shelter behind a fixed rock or wall to avoid the full force of the current.

HACK THIS: ESCAPE A CANYON

Stuck in a slickrock ravine? Use these techniques to get to safety.

1. **Flat-footing:** When ascending, descending, or traversing angled slabs, place the entire sole of your shoe on the rock. Slightly bend your knees and keep your weight over your feet to maximize friction.

2. **Stemming:** To climb over obstacles (boulders, water holes) or descend drops in narrow slots, scissor your legs and push them into opposite walls. Press your hands into each wall and move your feet up one at a time. Repeat. The opposing friction acts like brakes.

3. **Chimneying:** Move upward in a very narrow slot by pressing your back, hands, and butt against the wall behind you. Push both feet against the facing wall. Slide your back and butt up, then step your feet up to match. Repeat.

HACK THIS: CLIFFED OUT WITHOUT A ROPE

Improvising a rope is always sketchy and should never be your first choice. But in a survival situation here's how you do it.

Use the longest items you have handy. The longer the pieces, the fewer knots you'll need to hold them together, and knots equate to weakness. Ditto stitched seams. Cut your clothing or sleeping bag into strips and braid them. Join segments with a flat overhand knot. You need enough length to wrap your rope around a tree or rock and have both ends touch the ground below—or else you won't be able to retrieve it. Not long enough? Tie to an anchor using a bowline knot.

Now you'll need to stare into the abyss and master something called the Dülfersitz. Turn so your shoulders are perpendicular to the ledge and pass both strands (ideally) between your legs, around the downhill hip, over the opposite shoulder, and around the back of your neck. Grip the end with your downhill arm. The friction from all that surface area will leave you hollering for some Body Glide, but rope burn beats a dented head. (**Note:** Illustration shows real rope for positioning only.

Drowning

For something so critical to life, water poses a major threat when we have too much (or too little—see the Water chapter on pages 68-93). Here's a breakdown of what happens to the body when we can't get out.

➤ *Stuck in a slickrock ravine? Use these techniques to get to safety.* Credit: istockphoto

RESPIRATORY SYSTEM

When you're submerged, your respiratory system seizes up in seconds to prevent water from reaching the lungs. This instinct—the mammalian diving reflex—causes involuntary breath-holding and prevents you from making any sounds. Drowning is chillingly silent.

LARYNX

After a minute, your oxygen-starved brain will demand an inhale. The larynx—sensing the security breach—spasms, forcing the trachea to close in a last-ditch effort to protect the lungs. But it's only a twenty- to sixty-second stopgap. Many victims lose consciousness now.

HACK THIS: FLOAT WITH A TRASH BAG [OR YOUR PANTS]

Create two buoyancy chambers—and a place in-between to grab onto—by filling the bottom of a trash bag with air and cinching down the middle section with tape or cord. Then inflate the top of the bag with air and tie it closed. You can do this with your pants, too: Remove your pants, tie off the cuffs, grasp the open waistband, and plunge it top first into the water to fill the legs with air. The Red Cross teaches this when no better options exist, but it isn't foolproof: You may have to reinflate mid-swim.

11 RULES FOR CROSSING RIVERS

Forget bears and lightning: Runoff-swollen rivers pose one of the backcountry's biggest threats. Here's how to cross safely.

1. Look for a safer crossing if water is fast and knee-deep or deeper. Scout downstream of hazards like rapids, waterfalls, or fallen trees.
2. Always ford a river at its widest point, where the water will be shallower and slower.
3. Check your map for forks or braids, which split the river, reducing the volume of water.
4. Cross glacial rivers early in the day when possible, to avoid the higher runoff volume that comes with afternoon melting.
5. In muddy or silty rivers, lob a rock into the current; a hollow "ker-plop" indicates deep, possibly dangerous water. If the rock moves downstream before sinking or you hear rocks rolling downstream, don't ford—the current is too powerful.
6. Wear sandals or water shoes to improve footing. It's better to get your boots wet than take a risk going barefoot in tricky terrain.
7. Unbuckle your hip belt and sternum strap before fording fast-moving rivers so you can easily shed your pack if needed.
8. Use trekking poles or sticks to improve balance and probe ahead.
9. In strong current, cross at a slight angle, heading downstream but facing up. Lean a little into the current and step sideways.
10. For a difficult crossing, ford as a group with arms locked. For three people, form a tripod (everyone facing in). Alternatively, tie a rope to a tree and send a strong hiker across to tie off the other end. The last member brings the rope.
11. If you fall and the current takes you, flip on your back with your feet downstream. Ditch your pack if necessary and swim to shore as quickly as possible.

LUNGS

When the larynx relaxes, water floods the lungs. Known as "wet drowning," this reaction causes more than 90 percent of drowning deaths. Even if it doesn't kill, aspirated water permanently scars lung tissue. Survivors often report experiencing a chronic pattern of irregular breathing and coughing.

BLOOD

The circulatory system redirects up to 75 percent of your blood (your body's last oxygen supply) to your brain via the lungs. Starved of oxygen, the blood thins and becomes polluted with carbon dioxide bubbles, which build up and damage skeletal and muscular tissue within minutes.

BRAIN

Brain cells begin dying within four minutes of oxygen deprivation, meaning that even if you pull through, you risk losing pieces of your motor cortex. Near-drowning-related brain damage leaves survivors with a lifetime of headaches, blackouts, and poor coordination.

If you're smart, you never leave home without one. Now put it to use to ensure you always make it back.

FLAG DOWN RESCUERS

Flash your light in groups of three to indicate distress. If you're in a wooded area, tie the headlamp to the end of a long stick to reach over vegetation. Wave it to create a visible arc. Out of battery? Tap lightly around the side of the lamp with a sharp rock to separate the silver cup behind the bulb. Use the cup to reflect sunlight.

CATCH FISH

If your batteries die or you can't ignore your hunger, repurpose reflective elements to attract fish. Work the silver LED backing loose by pressing the edge of the disc with a sharp rock. Then smash the headlamp casing and fashion a gorge hook from a shard of sharpened plastic. Braid thread from the headband for a serviceable fishing line. Rather keep your lamp intact? Though illegal in some states under normal circumstances, holding a light over the water at night will attract plenty of species and lure them to a waiting hook or net.

START A FIRE

Strip and splice wires from the guts of the lamp until you can touch the ends to either terminus of a double-A or triple-A battery. (A partial charge will do.) This shorts the battery, turning the wire red-hot with electrical current. Use it to ignite tinder, but beware: Shorted batteries are prone to small but sudden explosions. Wear gloves and glasses if you can.

REPAIR GEAR

The lamp's plastic casing is just a little whittling away from becoming a sturdy needle. Break it open with a rock and use a knife to hone splinters into sewing tools. Use your needle to work loose nylon strands from the headband to use as thread.

TREAT INJURIES

The elastic headband can double as a compression bandage or hold a splint in place.

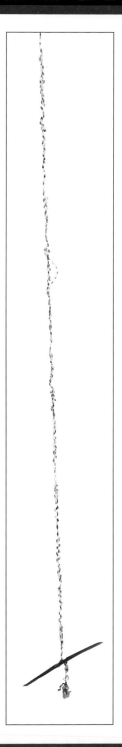

MAULED BY A GRIZZLY

BY TODD ORR

// WHEN I TURNED AROUND AND SAW THE SOW BARRELING TOWARD ME FOR THE SECOND TIME, I FIGURED MY LUCK HAD RUN OUT.

I had started from a trailhead in the Madison Valley near Ennis, Montana, an hour before sunrise. I was planning on a 15- to 20-mile loop around Sphinx Mountain. I grew up around here and had worked these mountains for the last twenty-five years as a trail engineer for the Custer Gallatin National Forest. I knew the terrain, the wildlife, and to always be prepared, especially for bears. I had my pistol in a shoulder holster and my bear spray on the sternum strap

eyes met, and within a second, her dark gray-brown body disappeared up the ridge into the trees. Her cubs followed.

I calmed myself. I'd seen dozens of bears react like this in my life, and assumed she was fleeing. A mother grizzly wasn't likely to abandon her cubs to pursue me, I reasoned, so I caught my breath, settled my nerves, and waited a minute before continuing, hiking away from her on another trail.

But just a few strides later, I heard brush crashing down behind me. I turned and saw 300 pounds of grizzly running down the ridge straight toward me. My hand pulled the safety pin of my bear spray and fired. I'd picked up the instinct training and working in bear country without a gun. But in two seconds, she burst through the cloud, 10 feet in front of me. I dropped onto my stomach and protected the back of my head and neck with my arms. She jumped onto my back, her front paws digging into my waist as she ground my body into the dirt. She tore into my right shoulder and arm half a dozen times until, fifteen seconds later, she left.

One Attack Down . . .

I laid there in shock and disbelief. Had I just survived a grizzly attack? I could feel the sting of open wounds oozing blood all over my back. Cautiously, I stood up. My wounds seemed

of my backpack, and I was yelling "Hey, bear!" every thirty seconds into the predawn darkness.

As the sun brightened the sky and touched the tops of the pines, I switched my flashlight off and continued up the well-worn path, no longer feeling the need to call out. Pushing forward, up and into a clearing, I halted. Some 80 yards away, a full-grown grizzly sow was playing with her cubs in the meadow I had just entered. Our

➤ Credit: Todd Orr

minor enough that I could walk. I didn't linger. Bears hardly ever attack twice, but I didn't want to test this one.

Adrenaline pumped through my blood and propelled me down the trail. I glanced nervously behind me every minute to make sure I was alone. Each step away from the attack eased my mind, and I realized how lucky I was to have escaped.

Eight or so minutes later, I was moving down the trail by a stream. The rushing water was loud—but not loud enough to block out the ominous sound of a large creature crashing through brush. I turned again to see the same grizzly charging toward me. She was already just 20 feet away, leaving me no time to grab my bear spray or my pistol.

She threw me to the ground and attacked again, her bites harder and deeper this time. Huddled in the same position as before, I felt the first bite on my left arm and heard the bone crunch between her teeth. As she ripped the tendons out of my arm, I gasped in pain. It made her attack harder. She bit me twenty or thirty times, lifting me up a few inches from the ground and slamming me back down, pushing me with her paws. Her claws dug into my back as I fought with all my might to stay still and silent. I knew my only chance was to play dead and wait for her to leave. While she ripped my pistol and binoculars off and trashed my day pack, I remained a statue, trying not to breathe. I focused on staying on my stomach; if she flipped me, I knew she'd kill me.

My other senses were heightened—the sound of her teeth on my bones, the smell of my blood. In my head, I kept telling myself she was going to leave. *She wants to go back and check on her cubs. Quit moving and play dead, and she will go away.* I used every bit of strength I had to stay motionless, and her biting slowed down. She sniffed, then bit. Sniffed, then bit. A

> "ADRENALINE PUMPED THROUGH MY BLOOD AND PROPELLED ME DOWN THE TRAIL."

minute passed until I felt the pressure on my chest release. She was gone.

Bloody Mess

I laid with a gash in my head leaking blood into my eyes, too afraid to move. I listened until I couldn't hear her anymore, then I pulled my hand slowly away from the back of my neck and reached for the pistol on my shoulder holster. Not there. Wiping the blood out of my eyes, I lifted my gaze from the ground to look around. I spotted my sidearm 10 feet away. I jumped up to grab it and my backpack, and set off immediately down the trail to get as much distance between myself and the bear as possible. I didn't second-guess what I should or shouldn't do, I just ran.

I examined my body as I moved down the trail—deep holes all over my back, shoulders, and arms. I could see blood dripping from my elbows, but nothing appeared to be gushing. Jacked up on adrenaline, I covered the remaining 3 miles in about forty-five minutes and arrived at the truck, where I found another car parked beside me. I pulled my phone out and shot a video telling people to be safe in the area, and then posted it to Facebook. I got in my car and drove the 17 miles to the Madison Valley Medical Center.

> ## "I EXAMINED MY BODY AS I MOVED DOWN THE TRAIL— DEEP HOLES ALL OVER MY BACK, SHOULDERS, AND ARMS."

When I walked in, everyone stared at me wide-eyed. There was a 5-inch flap of scalp hanging over my ear, and I think they were worried I'd panic if I knew how bad it looked.

My wound tally included twenty puncture wounds on my right arm and shoulder; two severed tendons, nerve damage, and shredded muscles in my left arm; that 5-inch gash above my right ear; and puncture wounds from the grizzly's teeth and claws on my back and waist areas.

I was lucky that I got away, but unlucky that she barreled through the bear spray and that she attacked twice. (**Note:** Bear spray is effective in deterring a grizzly attack in about 90 percent of cases.) But I was prepared. I don't second-guess my instinct to use the bear spray instead of the sidearm, but I wonder if the outcome would have been different. Even after years of experience dealing with wildlife, one thing you can't predict is how you'll react in the moment.

8

MIND GAMES

t's all in your head. When things go bad, your brain is not always your ally but there are ways to train it to work in your favor.

Judging by the advice elsewhere in this book, you may think simply reading about survival strategies will sufficiently prepare you for a survival situation. You'd be wrong. When faced with a real life-or-death situation, your brain's primary response is to disregard everything you've learned and revert instead to something primitive and instinctive: what you might call your lizard brain.

Emotional, reactive brain responses—the kind you have when under duress—follow different pathways than normal, voluntary ones, and they're tied much more closely to physical action. At the center of these emotional pathways sits a small area of the brain called the amygdala. Think of it as a paranoid and twitchy little man sitting in a bunker waiting for the world to end. If he perceives anything threatening, he throws the switch on a complex series of physical and chemical reactions commonly known as the fight-or-flight response.

But here's the rub: In a survival situation, this automatic response can help—or hurt—you. I know a woman who was swimming while on vacation in Mexico when an 8-foot saltwater crocodile took her head in its jaws—a situation no one prepares for. She responded automatically, struggling, screaming, and fighting. She escaped. By contrast, I knew an experienced stunt pilot who was arriving at her home airport when she saw that the landing wasn't going well. She reflexively pulled back the stick, stalled, and crashed. The defensive response cost her her life.

That doesn't mean it's not possible to train fight-or-flight. With enough practice, we can hack our brains to create new neural pathways that condition our minds and bodies to behave in certain ways. But it's important to realize the consequences and power of these pathways. I often think of the FBI agent who trained himself to grab a gun out of an assailant's hand. He practiced the motion, drilling it into his head and muscle memory. One day, he found himself face-to-face with an armed bad guy. He snatched the gun away. Then gave it back. His automatic pathway took over, so his brain did the exact action he'd trained it to do: Snatch the gun, hand it back, try again. Lucky for him, his partner was there to help.

Fortunately, you can properly develop your emotional responses by understanding the limited—but important—role reason plays in your reactions. Read up on your subject (i.e., the rest of this book) to inform the more modern and rational parts of the brain, but then let repetitive and stressful skills training shape those ancient emotional pathways that got us all from the caves to here.

And lastly, when you're in the thick of it, stay calm and be aware that both of these pathways need to work together. That way, the paranoid little man in your brain's bunker doesn't get all the votes on whether to flip the switch.
—Laurence Gonzales, author of *Deep Survival*

➤ *Hang on. Don't panic.* Credit: istockphoto

// PANIC ROOM: FIGHT, FLIGHT, OR CALM?

If there's one universal piece of survival advice, it's this: Don't panic. Panic makes irrational idiots out of otherwise reasonable people. In short, panic kills.

But here's the thing: You need panic. In a more positive light, we call it the fight-or-flight response, a highly automatic process that prepares the body for extraordinary feats of speed and strength. But panic can also cloud your judgment, leading to stupid—maybe fatal—decisions.

You may be hardwired for fight-or-flight, but if you recognize the signs of a freak-out, you can take steps to control it. A six-step process kicks off the body's fight-or-flight response, prepping you for action. Here's how to recognize each of those steps, and troubleshoot your own body's reaction (or overreaction) so you can hack your way out of a dangerous situation.

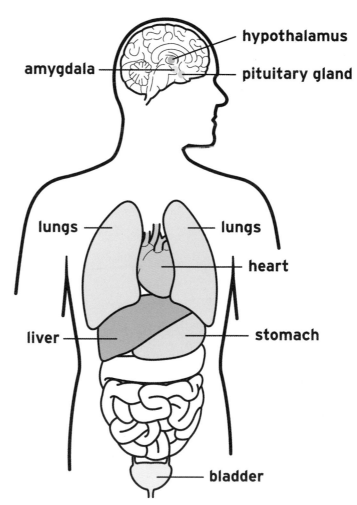

1. **Eyes and ears** start the panic response: You observe something that registers as a threat.
2. **The amygdala.** The threat message goes straight to this primitive region, the brain's main processing center for emotions—especially fear.
3. **Hypothalamus.** The amygdala signals this tiny region, which commands the fight-or-flight response.
4. **Pituitary gland.** When this gland receives the fear message from the hypothalamus, it releases hormonal signals to activate the adrenal glands.
5. **The adrenal glands** flush the hormone epinephrine (aka adrenaline) into the bloodstream.
6. **The circulatory system** swiftly moves epinephrine throughout the body, redirecting all functions to the immediate business of survival—and prompting the following bodily reactions simultaneously.

   > ➤ **The heart** speeds up and blood pressure rises, the better to direct blood to vital organs.
   > ➤ **The lungs** expand small airways to maximize air intake, and breathing rate spikes to deliver extra oxygen to the brain, boosting alertness.
   > ➤ **The liver** releases a store of glucose to supply the muscles with energy.
   > ➤ Blood shunts from **the stomach**, leaving behind the "butterflies" sensation.
   > ➤ **Sweat glands** open and muscles contract, making hair stand on end.
   > ➤ The walls of **the bladder** relax, which can lead to major embarrassment if the "threat" turns out to be a squirrel.

// REWIRING YOUR SURVIVOR'S BRAIN

Using your mind to override your body's autonomic responses and derail panic is only the first half of the survival equation. Once you've calmed the body, you'll need to change the way you *think* to stay in the survivor's mindset amidst trying

HACK THIS: STAY CALM

It sounds easy, and it's probably the most recommended piece of advice for adrenalized survival scenarios. But in practice, saying "stay calm" doesn't actually help you do that. Instead, commit these steps to memory and run through them like a checklist.

Stop. Panicked people tend to press on blindly, worsening their situation. In all but the most split-second dangers, you can afford to put on the brakes. I've done it when coming face-to-face with a bear, discovering I was profoundly lost, and when I climbed into something I wasn't sure I could climb out of. In all three situations, that extra moment of stillness gave me the chance to get closer to the right course of action (and the ability to be alive to write this book—bonus!).

Breathe. Counteract your body's instinct to hyperventilate by inhaling and holding your breath for a count of three. Similarly, deep breaths followed by a three-count exhale can counteract the short, shallow breathing that often slides into panic mode.

Focus. Keep your mind from spiraling out of control by zeroing in on a task. Baby steps—the right ones—can add up to increased safety and increased chances of success. If you spot that bear, observe its behavior and body language and concentrate on not running. Holding your ground shows the bear that you can defend yourself. Wait for it to react, or move away.

If you're lost, scan the area for useful landmarks in your current location. Sit down, have a drink and a snack, assess how far you might be from a road and how much water you have.

If you're cliffed out, make sure your current footing and position are stable and safe; if they aren't, take action to get comfortable and safe. Don't look down: Instead, take three deep breaths, find solid footholds and handholds (in that order), and slowly scurry out of danger. Add up enough small, smart steps and guess what: You'll eventually reach safety.

and changing conditions. Lucky you: The experts have a plan. The following recommendations offer proof-positive ways to alter thinking and behavior patterns in crisis situations. Some are simple, easy-to-remember ideas you can practice and play when out on the trail (like finding your survival mantra). Others are skills you won't test until the bottom drops out and you're playing with live ammo.

Confidence Game: Stay Positive, Stay Alive

In his twenty-five years as a Grand Canyon search-and-rescue ranger, Bil Vandergraff has logged 3,600 missions in the busiest national park for rescues, 10,000 backcountry patrol miles, and more than a few choice bits of wisdom on saving the injured. His most important survival skill? Confidence.

On rescues, Vandergraff deals with people who say "I can't" more than anything else. Hikers in distress insist they can't hike out, that they can't keep going even though their legs, arms, and lungs still work. The problem is their brain.

While physical training and wilderness skills are important for backpacking in difficult terrain, Vandergraff places equal importance on being able to psychologically escape the canyon. Anticipate possible difficulty and have confidence in your ability to solve your own problems.

Many Grand Canyon visitors come off the couch thinking hiking downhill is easy. Once they complete the 5,000-foot descent from rim to river, they quickly get overwhelmed by feeling physically trashed. Instead of simply resting, nursing their blisters, and adjusting their trip itinerary to fit a new reality, many of these shaken hikers immediately call for rescue. But park rangers aren't babysitters; they aren't even mandated to respond to distress calls within park boundaries (though they usually do).

Before you jam that distress button on your beacon, take stock of your situation. Assess your condition. Behave as if rescue isn't coming, and evaluate the steps you might take to self-rescue. Log your own strengths and weaknesses, and match rescue options to your strengths and risks to your current weaknesses. Dehydrated? Maybe plan on staying out an extra night to take advantage of a nearby water

> *Bil Vandergraff* Credit: Nick Cote

source. If your ankle is sprained but you otherwise have energy and adequate supplies, consider taking it extremely slow, but hiking yourself out.

Vandergraff tries to convince those who can hike to do so—and he insists they almost always make it. They even send him thank-you letters saying so.

Finding a Mantra: Words to Live By

Developing a mantra—which means "instrument of thinking" in Sanskrit—can help steer you away from negative thoughts. "Mantras help overcome your tendency to focus on pain, and instead concentrate your attention on the positive aspects of the here and now, while maintaining focus on the target: survival," says Dr. Rob Bell, a sports psychology coach. Here are the phrases that carried seven survivors through epic tough times.

"Amazing Grace, how sweet the sound . . ." —Linda Forney, hiker, 1975. She became disoriented on a short Grand Canyon hike and spent twenty days alone with no food and little water. On a stormy night, she kept her spirits up by singing "Amazing Grace."

"Pizza, french fries, pizza, french fries." —Jens Holsten, mountaineer, 2013. Holsten uses this phrase to propel himself home after excruciatingly tough expeditions, including establishing a new route on Denali.

"Man of action." —Yossi Ghinsberg, backpacker, 1981. After a rafting accident, he became separated from his companions in the Amazon rainforest and spent three weeks alone, struggling with rotting feet and surviving on wild fruit.

"Just have one more try—it's dead easy to die. It's the keeping-on-living that's hard." —Douglas Mawson, explorer, 1913. After falling into a crevasse in Antarctica, he recalled these words from Robert Service's poem "The Quitter."

"You'll make it because you have to." —Roberto Canessa, rugby player, 1972. The nineteen-year-old trekked through the Andes for ten days after the crash of Uruguayan Air Force Flight 571 to alert rescuers to the remaining sixteen survivors. He made it, and rescuers were able to locate his teammates.

"Keep going. Look how far you've gone. Just do it, don't think about it." —Joe Simpson, climber, 1985. He shattered his leg in the Peruvian Alps, and his climbing partner was forced to cut the rope. Simpson survived a 150-foot fall and crawled 5 miles back to camp, an inner voice spurring him on.

"Just hang on. That's all you can do." —Aron Ralston, canyoneer, 2003. While trapped in a Utah slot canyon for 127 hours, he clung to images of friends and family, and eventually escaped after amputating his own arm.

"_____." —Now it's your turn.

// COLLISION COURSE: AVERTING CRISIS

The best way to survive a disastrous set of circumstances? Don't fall into those circumstances in the first place. But that's harder than it sounds: Even outdoor professionals fall into traps they can't get out of when they stop balancing the weight of choices against the ever-changing environment and circumstances that define wilderness. Here's how to stay one (or three) steps ahead.

➤ *Stop, think, gather a plan.* Credit: istockphoto

Commitment-Phobe: Breaking Up with Danger

In 1976, psychologist Barry Staw coined the term "escalating commitment" to describe how individuals, organizations, and even governments lock themselves into a course toward disaster despite the fact that the outcomes have been consistently negative. It's how countries with all the information in the world get into intractable wars, and it's how experienced outdoorspeople don't act to extract themselves from catastrophic danger until it's too late. Two famous examples: The 1996 Everest tragedy (famously chronicled in Jon Krakauer's *Into Thin Air*) saw several separate teams swallowed by a storm after escalating mistakes; in 2012, several of the country's top skiers got caught in the monstrous Tunnel Creek avalanche after missing warning signs, ignoring concerns, and group-thinking their way into dangerous conditions.

But if you can pay attention to three key factors, both in the planning stages *and* during your trip, you have a better shot at avoiding disaster.

1. **Optimism and illusions of control.** Humans like to believe everything is going to work out just fine—it feels good and can lead to positive outcomes. But it also fuels false confidence and can make luck feel like skill. "They see themselves as performing better than others in most situations and able to avoid future mishaps," writes Staw. "Accidents and illness are things that happen to other people. Underlying such optimism is the belief that one can control one's destiny."

2. **Self-justification.** After having made a decision, "people convince themselves that it was the right thing to do," Staw says. This is particularly dangerous for trip leaders, who might refuse to second-guess incorrect moves, and less-expressive trip members, who might be afraid to challenge a leader's decision.

3. **Sunk costs.** After having devoted enormous resources of time, money, and emotion into a project, no matter how irrational it may be to continue, some people just can't bear to pull out. This shifts unearned value on factors (money, time) that can compromise more salient values (weather, risk).

5 RULES FOR TURNING BACK

Crappy weather, a throbbing knee, low food: Any one of these could be a legit reason to head home. But much of the satisfaction and essence of outdoor adventure comes from meeting challenges head-on and overcoming them. Being able to tell the difference is one of the toughest mental tasks in the outdoors. The next time you face one of these dilemmas, ask yourself these five questions.

1. **Are you safe and comfortable?**
   Fear, hunger, thirst, fatigue, even cold feet affect your ability to make a good decision. If you answered "no" to this question, stop and fix the problem before you make any big decisions.

2. **Are you under pressure to achieve this goal?**
   You don't have to be a pro to feel pressed to succeed. The cost of the trip, status with friends, inability to return and try again, work obligations, pride—all of these factors can influence your decision.

3. **What happens if you turn around?**
   Sometimes retracing your steps is easy; other times it means hard work and extra time, which can make you reluctant to retreat even if it's the smart thing to do.

4. **What happens if you continue forward?**
   What is the biggest risk? Could you die or will you just be late and uncomfortable?

5. **What do you do when you just don't know?**
   In some situations, you might ask yourself the first four questions and still find yourself with no clear answer. Don't flip a coin. Ask yourself what rescuers would say if you kept going and something terrible happened. Will they say you were unlucky—or an idiot?

Talk Your Way to Safety

You're in risky terrain, and you've identified risk factors, but you're in a group. How to proceed? Matt Schonwald of BC Adventure Guides practices something he calls "Conversation-Fu" to differentiate useful communication from harmful conversation, with the aim of making safe choices in an environment where some acceptance of risk is just part of the deal. "Whether guiding or with friends, I practice it every day I'm in the outdoors," he says. "I'm engaging others in the conversation of risk. Every accident has poor communication one way or the other—so if you improve communication, you might improve the outcome." Here's an example of how that might happen in an actual conversation.

That looks dangerous. "This comes off as bluster that puts people on opposite sides: You either feel comfortable with that assessment or you don't. That's the hardest thing about risk: People try to psyche themselves up for a challenge rather than admit and discuss the consequences. This is the opportunity for everyone in the group to present objective data and be heard equally before you make a decision, and be as honest as possible."

We made it all this way. We're here, so let's do it. "When you work hard to get to an objective, there's a cognitive bias that obscures things like changing conditions. Be honest with yourself, because nature won't lie. It may be complex or hard to understand, but it'll tell you everything you need to pay attention to."

So are we doing it? Yes or no? "Nature is not a binary his/her, yin/yang, caring/not caring thing. It's a vacuum filled with lots of variables, and we're just one piece of it. No matter how beautiful it is, or how cool the animal encounter, you need to see it the way nature sees you: as one of many animals and factors moving around in space at any given moment. Understanding that and assessing that realistically is part of getting to know the land on an intimate level, which enriches the whole outdoors experience—even if you have to turn back."

Sure, a big pull of Kentucky's finest might calm your nerves in a dire situation. But you can put it to even better use with these tips for starting a fire, treating water, and even signaling for help.

SIGNAL FOR HELP

Survival guru Tony Nester suggests tying a bandanna or shoelace around the bottle's neck, then hanging the bottle somewhere elevated, like a tree branch. The key is to get it off the ground, so you expose more surface area and maximize glint. This passive signaling method also frees you up to perform key tasks like building shelter. Any shiny object will work: bottles, mirrors, space blankets, hubcaps, bike parts, even a machete.

START A FIRE

To make wood more flammable, whiskey-soak it to the core, then wait a few minutes so the vapors disperse, reducing the risk of a fireball. In damp conditions, resinous woods (pine, spruce, fir, mesquite)—which have a lower ignition point—work best; avoid oak and maple.

Nester also suggests filling a small can (like a tuna or Altoids can) with whiskey and lighting it. Or you can

build a sand fire by scooping a cupful of dirt into a mound (it must be a dry substrate like sand, or clay formed into a small clay pinch pot). Then pour in a quart of whiskey. It should burn ten to thirty minutes; as the flame dies, use a stirring stick to bring fuel back to the surface and add a few minutes of life. Although your sand fire won't be hot enough to boil water, it can provide warmth, heat food, or help light a signal fire. For the latter, feed in twigs, then transfer the burning twigs to a fire pit. (Beware of wildfire hazard in dry backcountry areas.)

If you don't have a lighter, pour out the whiskey, fill the bottle with water, and start a fire magnifying-glass style. With the sun at its zenith (11 a.m. to 2 p.m.), focus the sun's beams onto some rotten, punky wood, dry cow pies, or dry elk droppings until you get a glowing ember. Nestle this in grass or dry bark, then blow it into a flame. If the bottle has broken, try a shard: Add one or two beads of liquid, then lie flat with your forearms supported, focusing the beam as per above, with the water-droplet side facing the sun. You must let the pinpoint of light concentrate for

twenty to thirty seconds on the tinder before it will ignite, so keep still and be patient.

CARE FOR CUTS

Now imagine you're injured—does the old cowboy "whiskey in the wound" method work? Modern liquor, including bourbon, clocks in at 40 percent alcohol—only half the punch of the Wild West moonshines—but it still kills topical germs. It might also kill healthy cells, however, and it burns like hell, making clean water a better option. Whiskey does work to sterilize instruments and to blunt pain—drinking two ounces of 90-proof George Dickel reduces pain roughly 50 percent for two hours, according to our tester.

TREAT IFFY WATER

Early settlers in Canada's Red River area who mixed a little whiskey into their drinking water had fewer incidences of waterborne illness than their counterparts. Add a shot to your liter of water, then wait twenty minutes. You want dead—not drunk—giardia.

ATTACKED IN THE WOODS

BY DAVID STEPHEN WINGFIELD

> // **KYLE'S BODY PREPPED ITSELF FOR FIGHT OR FLIGHT, LOOSENING WHAT COULD BE LOOSENED. THE NON-SCIENTIFIC COMMUNITY HAS A SPECIFIC TERM FOR THIS CONDITION: SCARED SHITLESS.**

2:05 a.m.; *Dismal Falls, Virginia*

My dad woke to the sound of something rustling against the tent. Something big. It's a bear, he thought. Time slowed. My dad thought about life, his wife, and his son, who slept beside him and who might die with him on this lonesome night at Dismal Falls. My dad is a man of action.

Hey!" he screamed. "Get out!"

He rolled onto his side and started punching the bear though the wall of the tent. His fists

"HE ROLLED ONTO HIS SIDE AND STARTED PUNCHING THE BEAR THOUGH THE WALL OF THE TENT."

was to camp at the Dismal Falls campground. It was an arbitrary destination for us, but one with a grim history: A few years back, a crazy person shot two hikers who were staying there, wounding them. (The guy was subsequently caught and went to jail.)

When you're hiking in the woods with family and friends, you try not to think about that sort of thing, but sometimes it's hard to think about anything else. I asked Kyle, "Remember that guy who shot those people at Dismal?"

"The Dismal Falls we're hiking to?"

"They were just wounded," my dad interjected.

We walked on in a heavy silence of three men waiting for the gallows. The mood was dark by the time we arrived at Dismal Falls.

A knee-deep stream cuts through the camping area, leading to the namesake falls, a noisy 12-footer. We shared supper with another hiker, Bob, who required strong hearing aids to converse (and infrequently used them). After supper, Bob put in his hearing aids to say he would "set up on the far side of this creek" and "see you guys in the morning." Kyle pitched his one-man tent on the near side of the creek, and Dad and I put our two-man 20 yards farther downstream.

Dad set up the sleeping gear while I bear-bagged the food. When I got back, I found Dad in his bag with the feet-end downhill. I reminded

slammed into the thick animal, but the bear wouldn't leave. I yelled, "Dad!" and his son's voice gave him a surge of paternal strength. He gave the bear everything he had. "Git!" he shouted. "Get out of here!"

Earlier That Day

It was summer, and my dad and I were on our annual section hike on the Appalachian Trail. One of my coworkers, Kyle, had joined us. Our plan him that I like to sleep with my feet uphill so the blood drains out and they don't become sore.

There was grumbling. It's one thing to walk 14 miles in a day with twenty-five pounds strapped on your back—it's another thing entirely to get back up when you're already in your bag. So I changed tactics, asking if he had done his last pee. (Nobody wants to wake up in the middle of a good sleep just to go pee in the cold.)

There was more grumbling, but the seed was planted—he had to go. While he did his "safety pee," I turned our bags the way I like them: feet uphill. He came back and didn't seem to notice. The grumbling slowly changed to snoring.

2:08 a.m.
Kyle woke shortly after 2 a.m. to hear four shouts in the Dismal darkness: "Hey!"

. . . "Get out!" . . . "Git!" . . . "Get out of here!" Then silence, the eternal rushing of water, and the roar of his heart. The Dismal Falls killer was back. Kyle's body prepped itself for fight-or-flight, loosening what could be loosened. The non-scientific community has a specific term for this condition: scared shitless.

Kyle scrambled out of his tent and yanked down his white spandex thermals to meet his body's response as best he could. He perched there, frozen in fear, as he strained to hear any clues as to the killer's whereabouts or further intentions. But he didn't want to die here, not like this. He stood, pulled up his spandex, switched

" . . . GET OUT! . . . GIT! . . . GET OUT OF HERE! "

on his headlamp, and waded barefoot across the creek. *Bob might be dead*, he thought. He swept his light across the tent expecting slash marks and blood. Nothing. *Maybe Bob is OK.*

"Bob?!" he called. No response.

Bob is dead. Kyle crept around the tent, inspecting each side with his light.

The tent was fine. Then it moved.

2:06 a.m.
Something was hitting me in the ribs. Hard. I heard my dad scream, "Get out!" and he socked me again.

"Dad!" I yelled. My dad used to be a cop and even in his sixties he's no softy.

"Git!" he yelled. I struggled to free myself from the mummy bag.

"Dad! Stop!"

"Get out of here!" my dad screamed, punctuating each word with a fist. With one arm pinning me down, he turned and shouted over his shoulder, "There's a bear!"

He must be dreaming. "Wake up!" I freed my hands and tried to block his punches.

My father hissed, "I am awake!" The wild whites of his eyes glimmered in the darkness. This was no dream.

My universe imploded—my father was insane. After a lifetime of love, it came down to one night in a tent. One of us would get out alive. The door was on his side. There was no choice: I had to fight.

I rolled into him with my body to shorten his punches. "There. Is. No. Bear." I grabbed his wrist and pinned it to his body.

"Then what has my arm?"

"I do!"

His body relaxed.

"There's no bear. It's me."

A short silence ensued as my world realigned itself along the familial axis.

"I'M GLAD YOU DIDN'T GET UP IN THE MIDDLE OF THE NIGHT TO PEE OUT THE DOOR."

"I guess you seemed like a bear."

And then my dad started to chuckle. It was infectious. Turns out there's a lot to laugh about once your dad stops trying to kill you.

"You can really hit," I told him when I caught my breath.

"Sorry. I thought the door was on my left side."

"I turned the bags around when you did your last pee."

"Oh."

"I'm glad you didn't get up in the middle of the night to pee out the door."

He agreed. "You're lucky I was just trying to kill you."

"Do you think Kyle heard us yelling?"

"If he's worried, he'll check on us."

2:30 a.m.
After being shooed away by a very alive (and very annoyed) Bob, Kyle waded back across the creek and crawled into his sleeping bag. He'd lie there awake and uncertain as he waited for the dawn.

The next morning, Kyle asked if we heard any strange noises during the night. I smiled. "Nothing strange."

"Really?" Kyle said, "I thought somebody was attacked."

"Well . . ."

HACK THIS: DENTAL FLOSS

If you follow dentist's orders and floss every night even while in the backcountry, your commitment to oral hygiene comes with a survival bonus. Single strands of floss can double as stitching or sewing material to mend both clothing and deep wounds. Meanwhile, you can weave several strands together to make cordage for fishing line, snares, bear bags, shelter rigging, or lashing your knife to a stick to make a spear. Remove the spool: An empty floss container is perfect for storing live bait like ants, grubs, worms, or crickets.

9

FITNESS

Should you ever be unlucky enough to fight for survival in the wild, it will demand all your strength—of mind, of skill, of body. We've addressed the first two, now don't neglect the third: your fitness. Hone your body, and be ready for anything.

In 2014, I went hiking in the Medicine Bow Mountains, near my home in Wyoming. Alone. I brought no cell phone or satphone or locator beacon, and told no one, not even my wife, where I was going. I slipped out of the house at 4 a.m., listened to the BBC while driving up to 11,000 feet, then set off on a 7-mile circuit that included two summits. At this elevation, in June, the landscape was still buried beneath a thick plate of snow, which made cross-country travel—at least early on a cold morning—easy and direct.

When I arrived at a high lake I had planned to cut straight across, I found it only partially frozen. Long blue leads of meltwater sliced across the white ice like crevasses. Nonetheless, I thought I could see a way to the distant shore. I stepped onto the ice and crunched out to the first lead, then turned right, tiptoeing along its edge until it narrowed enough for me to jump to the next jigsaw piece of ice. If I questioned the wisdom of proceeding like this alone, I don't recall it. The tactic worked, and I gradually zigzagged across the lake. However, on the far side I discovered I was stranded on the ice thanks to a crescent strip of open water separating me from the shoreline.

Going back the way I came was unacceptable. I'd made too many desperate leaps. I searched left and right, eventually finding a crust of ice that bridged over to the talus. It was clearly too thin to walk on, so I laid down on my stomach, dispersing my weight, and used the pick of my ice axe—stretched out in front of me in both hands—to pull myself forward.

This awkward, horizontal maneuver got me within 5 feet of shore before I heard a dreadful cracking sound and felt a shudder in the ice that went straight up into my guts. I had the briefest moment to contemplate my fate before I fell through the ice.

Falling through the ice on a frozen alpine lake, miles from help, is a classic hiker's nightmare. If you're alone, it is presumed that the cold water will instantly paralyze your body and your boots will fill with water, and you'll be helplessly dragged down into the shadowy depths, bubbles streaming from your mouth, your eyes slowly rolling back in your head.

In this event, I was simultaneously flailing valiantly with my ice axe as I was going under. The pick happened to stick into a sizable block of ice, and I managed to drag myself out of the freezing black water with remarkable alacrity. My head didn't even go under. I scrambled to shore, leapt to my feet, and shook like a dog. I was surprised to find myself no worse for wear—other than being thoroughly soaked and cold. Very cold. Both the air and the water temperature were barely above freezing. The thought of hypothermia (a miserable, self-inflicted condition I've had many times) flashed through my mind and briefly made me feel stupid for not having simply walked around the lake. What a silly way to go! But then, thankfully, my rational self spoke up: *Deal. Don't whine.*

With nothing but snow and rock for miles, building a fire was out of the question. And with no lovely lass with whom to strip naked, slip into a sleeping bag, and get deliciously rewarmed flesh-to-flesh (an obvious point against going solo, it must be said), my options were limited. I peeled off my gaiters, unlaced my boots, ripped off my pants, emptied the water out of my boots, wrung out my socks, wrung out my pants, and put them all back on in a matter of minutes. Then I struck off up the mountain at a pace so hellish it was certain to pump warm blood through my entire body.

Boot-kicking and swinging my ice axe rhythmically and ceaselessly, I ascended a 1,000-foot couloir in twenty minutes. By the time I reached the top my body was throwing off heat like a steam engine. My clothes? Dry.

Standing on the summit of this insignificant little mountain, I was glad that I'd left no word of my plans, that no one on earth knew my whereabouts. Had I told someone where I was going, there would have been a tether. Without it, I was free! It was just me and the mountain. Flesh and granite, ice and sky. Between my brush with hypothermia, and the fast ascent, and the knowledge that I was utterly alone, I felt so invigorated my heart almost lifted me off the ground.

Was it reckless to keep going upward in wet clothes in freezing temps? Would I have suffered Ralston-level ridicule if another accident had struck and I'd left myself no margin for safety? Probably. But I felt confident in my assessment of the conditions and my experience. Which brings up a critical component of smart solo travel: Know your limits. Without companions, you must think for yourself, make decisions for yourself, and be willing to bear the consequences on your own. You must know your abilities well enough to separate acceptable challenge from dangerous folly. This requires an internal truthfulness not often demanded of us in modern life. On your own in the wild, the threat of serious consequences sharpens the experience and intensifies decision-making. You become your only safety net; there is no plan B. —Mark Jenkins

// STRONG LIKE BULL: GET GUIDE-FIT FOR LIFE

Physical strength powers a trip, but mental strength keeps everything afloat when things go south. While caught without shelter on a survival trip, Bryan Pope, an instructor at Earth Native Wilderness School, became stranded without shelter in a cold November thunderstorm in near-freezing temps. To keep his core warm and ward off hypothermia, he marched from midnight to sunrise nonstop. "Knowing my body wouldn't fail enabled me to focus on the mental game staying warm and safe," he says.

How'd he do it? Through meticulous and integrated strength, flexibility, and cardio training that works every major muscle in your body. If you want to break your fitness plateau and be ready for anything, follow his routine six days a week. Best of all, anyone can do it. Beginners can start with no weights and walk or hike instead of run. (If you're just getting back into shape, try three days a week instead of six.)

"In the mornings I do core circuits every day, paired with either upper-body or lower-body circuits on alternating days," he says. Form is paramount: Weights shouldn't ever be more than fifteen pounds, and unless you're used to working out every day, start with no weights. For each alternating day, choose three exercises from below. For each, complete 3 sets of 20 reps. For each alternating day, choose three exercises from below. Take care to mix and match: Varying your routine and avoiding too much repetition builds muscle. "I usually do this in the morning and run or hike 3 to 7 miles in the evening, three days a week."

Lower/Core Circuit (x3)

QUADS/GLUTES

Sumo Squats: Stand with feet 3 to 4 feet apart and toes pointing out at a 45-degree angle. Bend your knees until your thighs are parallel with the floor, making sure not to let your knees extend past your toes.

    Side Walk with Exercise Band: Step inside an exercise band and stand with your feet shoulder-width apart. Lower into a squat with your knees at a 45-degree angle and take 10 steps to the right, then 10 steps to the left. Complete 3 sets of 20 reps.

HAMSTRINGS

Bird Dogs: Start on all fours with arms directly under your shoulders and knees directly under your hips. Extend your left arm forward and your right leg back so they are parallel with the floor. Repeat with right arm and left leg.

> Credit: Lauren Tedford

HIPS

Scissors: Lie on your back with legs straight and extended toward the ceiling. Lower your right leg as you lift your head and shoulders off the floor. When your right leg is only a few inches off the floor, lift it back to upright as you lower your left leg.

CALVES

Calf Raises: Stand on the edge of a raised platform (like a staircase or a heavy book) on the balls of your feet. Raise your heels until you are on your tiptoes, then lower your heels below the platform.

CORE/BACK

V-Ups: Lie on your back with your arms and legs extended parallel to the floor. Keep arms and legs straight as you lift your shoulders off the floor and touch your hands to your feet.

➤ Credit: Lauren Tedford

Beetles: Lie with your knees bent in the air at a 90-degree angle and your arms outstretched at 90-degree angles. Extend your right leg parallel to the floor as you touch your left foot with your right hand. Repeat on left side.

Upper/Core Circuit (x3)

CHEST

Push-Ups: Start with your hands on the floor directly below your shoulders and your toes curled under. Your arms and legs should be straight. Bend your arms until your body is only a few inches from the floor, being sure to keep your back and buttocks straight. Straighten your arms and repeat.

Single-Arm Chest Press: Lie on your back on a bench, holding a dumbbell above your head with your arm straight. Lower the dumbbell until your arm is at a 90-degree angle, with the bicep parallel to the floor.

➤ Credit: Lauren Tedford

BACK

Chin-Ups: Hang from a bar with arms straight, shoulder-width apart and knuckles facing away from you. Pull your body up until your elbows are completely bent and your face is above the bar. Lower until your body is straight again.

Reverse Flys: Lie on a 45-degree bench on your stomach with your arms extended perpendicular to your body. Keeping arms straight, move your arms outward to make a T.

SHOULDERS

Arm Circles: Stand with arms outstretched at your sides and parallel to the floor. Move your arms in a circular motion, first forward and then backward.

➤ Credit: Lauren Tedford

TRICEPS

Bench Dip: Sit on the edge of a bench with your hands gripping the edge and your arms shoulder-width apart. Push up off the bench so that your legs and arms are straight and your back is close to the bench. Lower your body until your elbows create a 90-degree angle.

BICEPS

Zottman Curls: Stand with arms straight by your sides and palms facing forward with dumbbells. Keep the upper arm straight and bend from the elbow to bring the dumbbells to your shoulders. If you only have one dumbbell, put your free hand on your hip.

➤ Credit: Lauren Tedford

CORE/BACK

Russian Twists: Sit with your knees bent and your upper body at a 45-degree angle with the floor. Lift your feet off the floor and twist to bring the dumbbell to one hip, then the other.

Supermans: Lie on the floor on your stomach with arms and legs extended straight. Keeping arms and legs straight, lift your chest and feet off the floor, then lower.

➤ Credit: Lauren Tedford

HACK THIS: THE 10-MINUTE FITNESS PLAN

OK, fine: Not all of us are going to go in for a life-changing, full-body workout simply under the pretense of gaining Superman or Wonder Woman's physique *just in case* you end up screwed in the backcountry. Work, family, and Netflix so often get in the way. But do you have ten minutes? Of course you do—and you can see surprisingly solid fitness gains in that amount of time with these exercises. Rob Shaul, founder of the Mountain Tactical Institute in Jackson, Wyoming, designed this workout for the time-pressed. Do it daily (alternating between maximum intensity and moderate intensity) and complete as many sets of the circuit as you can in ten minutes.

SCOTTY BOBS

Leg strength is important, but a strong upper body helps with pack comfort and stability on tricky terrain. Total body fitness is the key to success in the mountains, and this exercise works your arms, chest, back, and core simultaneously.

1. Start in plank position with a dumbbell in each hand (25 pounds for men, 15 for women).
2. Do a push-up.
3. Pause in the up position and do one dumbbell row (lift the weight to your shoulder elbow out and in line with your shoulder) with the right arm.
4. Repeat steps 1 to 3, using the left arm. This is 1 rep. Repeat for 3 reps.

STEP-UPS

This exercise mimics hiking uphill under a load, building power in your quads, hamstrings, and glutes. Whether you're day hiking or grinding out hundreds of miles, these muscles are the engines driving you.

1. Stand facing a 20-inch box. Leading with your right leg and driving off your left, step up onto the box with both feet.
2. Step backward off the box into your original position. This is 1 rep.
3. Repeat, leading with the left leg and driving off the right. Step down. Repeat for 12 reps, alternating the leading leg.

SHUTTLE RUNS

Hikers need aerobic fitness for steep hills and long days. This simple cardio workout gets you mountain-ready without having to spend hours on a treadmill. It also elevates your heart rate as you cycle back to the first two exercises, says Shaul, turning the whole circuit into a cardio challenge.

1. Set up two cones (or other objects) 40 feet apart.
2. Starting at one end, run from one cone to the other, going around them.
3. Complete 3 laps (cone to cone and back is one lap).

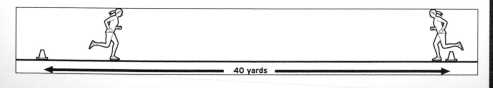

40 yards

3 RULES FOR STRONGER FEET

Your feet are literally your first point of contact with the wild. Stronger foot muscles can end ankle sprains and aching arches (and prevent the accidents that come from both). As you hike, the muscles in your feet and ankles flex and contract in an intricate series of mechanical movements. Most workouts don't target them, but like any muscles, you can improve them. This is especially important if you have unusually high or low arches. Perform the following exercises two to three times weekly.

1. **Towel pulls:** Place a towel on the floor with a book or 5-pound weight on one end. While seated, plant your bare heels on the other end of the towel and draw the weighted end of the towel toward you by curling it with your toes. Repeat 10 times.

2. **Ankle builders:** While standing or sitting, place a 4-foot length of heavy rubber tubing, elastic band, or bungee cord under the middle of your foot and grasp one end in each hand. To strengthen the inside of your ankle, pull on the side of the cord that's farthest from your big toe and resist with your ankle (called "inversion"). Hold for 5 seconds. To work the outside ankle muscles, pull on the side of the cord that's closest to your big toe and resist (called "eversion"). *Note:* Eversion strengthening is very helpful for people with a history of sprained ankles.

3. **Jump rope:** This exercise develops foot muscles along with leg muscles and the cardiovascular system. Start out jumping rope for 1 minute 3 times a week, then increase the length of the sessions by 1 minute per week thereafter, with the goal of a 15-minute routine.

HACK THIS: KNEE INJURIES

Knee injuries are one of the most common injuries hikers can experience in the backcountry. If you have weak knees or are recovering from a previous knee injury, focus on these exercises three times a week to build up your leg's all-important hinge.

- Lay a 10-foot-long 2 x 4 flat on the ground. Walk forward and backward on it for its full length, 10 times. No 2 x 4? Use a concrete curb or other roughly foot-wide structure that forces you to focus on balance.
- Stand on one foot and balance for 15 seconds, 10 times. Repeat with the other foot.
- Do 10 one-quarter squats on the injured leg, still standing on the 2 x 4 or curb. Repeat with the other leg.

// BALANCING ACT: SURE STEPS TO GET SURE-FOOTED

You want good balance for more than just hopping rocks and crossing log bridges. Boosting your balance goes a long way toward improving your stability on difficult terrain, thereby preventing injuries and getting you out of a tight spot. Here's how to gain the balance of a ballerina in the wild.

1. **Make balance exercises part of your regular training routine.** Practice a flamingo stance on stable ground (aim for 30 seconds) before progressing to a more dynamic surface like a balance disk, suggests James Fisher, an Arizona-based performance trainer of adventure athletes. Start with your lifted leg bent at 45 degrees (picture the *Karate Kid*). To increase difficulty, straighten it out to the front, back, or side of the weight-bearing leg.

2. **Try standing on one foot while doing chores.** One-legged dishwashing will boost domestic karma as well as core strength.

3. **Add backpacking-specific exercises.** After four weeks of stabilization training, Fisher suggests this variation on a workout staple: Step out of a lunge by straightening your front leg and bringing your back leg forward to 90 degrees, foot off the ground, thigh level with your hips. Easy? Add a weighted pack or try more powerful movements, like single-leg squats.

4. **Breathe for balance.** Failing to breathe is a surefire way to get derailed. Breathe slowly and regularly to keep muscles relaxed.

5. **Avoid vertigo by focusing on a fixed point.** Look for a spot 5 to 10 feet in front of you.

6. **Keep shoulders and hips squared to your destination and knees bent.** This will lower your center of gravity and quicken your reactions.

7. **Take small, slow steps.**

8. **Raise your arms overhead in the trickiest spots.** This allows for slighter shifting of body weight to reach a more precise equilibrium. Stay loose, with your arms in a U-shape; sway them side-to-side to adjust your balance.

9. **Get help.** If the terrain allows, use a trekking pole or sturdy stick to serve as a third point of contact.

Get Limber

Skip stretching, and you're missing out on a key element for staying efficient and injury-free on wilderness adventures. But there are two kinds of stretches to master: dynamic stretches (ideal for prehike warm-ups) and static stretches (great for post-exercise soreness and recovery). Learn when and how to do both.

DYNAMIC STRETCHES

Speedy and controlled movements that engage hiking muscles, dynamic stretches can help loosen and warm them up, and reduce your risk of injury when done before you hit the trail. Use momentum for quick movements, but actively use muscles to maintain control and aim for a warm-up of at least five minutes using these stretches.

> **Forward Leg Swing:** Stand alongside a wall or chair and swing or kick your outside leg. Increase your leg's swing until you're extending it as high as possible in front and behind. Do 10 to 15 swings on each side. Keep your upper body upright, and eyes straight ahead.

➤ Credit: Tegra Stone Nuess

> **Twisting Lunge:** From a standing position, lunge by extending your right leg and lowering your left knee to the ground with your back straight and shoulders back. Keep your hands in front of your body, and don't extend your knee beyond your toes. As you lunge, twist your upper body to the right. Do 10 to 12 per side.

> Credit: Tegra Stone Nuess

➤ **Butt Kicks:** Walk (or jog) approximately 10 yards, leaning forward slightly and staying on the balls of your feet. As you move forward, flex your knees and kick your heels up to your buttocks. Aim to fit 20 kicks in the 10-yard space.

➤ Credit: Tegra Stone Nuess

➤ **Walking High Knees:** Like marching, keep your body and legs in line, and take an exaggerated step forward, driving your right knee high and pushing up onto the toe of your left foot. Land flat-footed, without making any forward progress, then switch legs. Swing your arms (bent 90 degrees) and take 15 to 20 steps on each leg.

➤ Credit: Tegra Stone Nuess

STATIC STRETCHES

Holding a muscle under tension (the essence of static stretching) can reduce strength and muscle stability if done before a workout. But after a workout, static stretches elongate muscles and flush lactic acid to reduce next-day soreness. Don't hold tension for longer than thirty seconds, breathe while holding stretches, and don't hold at a point of discomfort.

> **Standing Quad Stretch:** Start by standing, feet together; use a chair or wall to steady yourself if you need. Bend your right leg and place your foot in your right hand, just behind your butt. Press your foot into your hand to stretch your quad and hold for 15 to 30 seconds. Repeat with your opposite leg several times.

> **Butterfly Stretch:** Sit straight and bend your knees while pulling your feet (soles together) toward your groin. Grab your feet and lift them slightly, using your elbows to hold your knees flat or down. Hold the inner-thigh stretch for 15 to 30 seconds.

> Credit: Tegra Stone Nuess

- ➤ **Hurdler's Stretch:** Sit straight-backed with legs outstretched, toes pointed straight up. Bend your right knee, placing your right sole against your left thigh. Bend forward from the hips, sliding your hands toward your ankle. Hold the stretch for 10 to 30 seconds and switch legs.
- ➤ **Standing Butterfly Stretch:** Stand straight with your feet wide apart (twice your shoulder width). Keeping your back straight, bend one leg and lower your body while keeping your feet parallel. Use your abs and arms to balance and hold yourself upright and hold for 10 to 30 seconds.

➤ Credit: Tegra Stone Nuess

Think duct tape is only good for patch jobs and covering blisters? Think again. The adhesive-of-the-gods can save more than your tent fly. The only limit to its usefulness is your imagination. Here are seven ways duct tape can save your butt in an emergency.

1. **Fight the cold.** Affix the tape to your boot liner to reflect the heat from your feet back toward your body. Pro tip: Some snow machine racers cover their faces in duct tape to protect their skin from the cold.

2. **Build a fire.** No dry tinder? Thanks to its cotton innards, duct tape ignites when exposed to a flame. A small roll of it will burn for twenty to thirty seconds.

3. **Craft a paddle.** Wrap the end of a forked stick tightly with duct tape. Tip: Cover the fork with a dry bag to improve performance and keep water from seeping through the layers of duct tape and weakening them.

4. **Signal for rescue.** Duct tape's reflective exterior can alert searchers. Make something they can see from the air: Think big (10-plus feet) and angular.

5. **Splint a broken arm or leg.** Create a splint by padding a branch with duct tape, stabilize a busted limb by wrapping it twice, or construct makeshift bandages.

6. **Twine a rope.** Double-back a strip of duct tape, sticking it to itself. Braid several of these together for added durability. In an emergency, use them to rappel a short cliff. (A three-strand rope held a 150-pound person in my test.)

7. **Make cordage.** Tear a long strip of duct tape in half lengthwise and roll the strand in your hand to make cord. Use this as the string on your fire bow.

UNDERWATER

BY GARY FERGUSON AS TOLD TO ALI HERMAN

// IT HAD BEEN A RELATIVELY TAME TRIP FOR THE FIRST 3 MILES, BUT NOW A 200-YARD STRETCH OF UNRUNNABLE RAPIDS LAY BEFORE US.

We pulled the boat over to scout the portage, unaware that a storm a few years back had drastically changed the river's banks. Instead of the easy passage we expected, we'd have to paddle dangerously close to the mouth of the rapids to reach the new portage point. Back in our 17-foot Old Town Tripper canoe, we paddled slowly toward the bank. The river had a different plan.

All of a sudden, 5-foot waves crashed into our canoe, and we tried to yell to each other over the roar. "Left!" then "Right, right, right!" There was no time to feel nervous; we concentrated on avoiding the boulders that obstructed our every move. We were in the maw of the rapids and there was nothing we could do about it.

We made it 100 yards before our canoe spiraled sideways and breached a large rock. The boat flipped immediately, pinning us in the icy water. Upside down, I reached for the Velcro straps holding my legs in the canoe and was free. The boat's hull crashed—like thunder—against massive granite boulders. I surfaced. There was no sign of Jane.

The current muscled me away from the canoe and down the river, twice dragging me under into recirculation pools. My life jacket was no match for the current. Massive amounts of pressure bore down on my body, holding me under. I thought it was the end. But by some miracle I returned to the surface. I was catapulted over a 5-foot waterfall, and my leg jammed into a large rock crevice. I heard it snap three times. The current spit me out and I got kicked, face up, into a 40-yard flush pond at the end of the rapids. There was still no sign of Jane.

A Lifetime of Experience

Jane and I met in college and had been married twenty-five years. We were constant wilderness companions. We traveled all over North America and into the Arctic, hiking and paddling. To hone our skills, we decided to spend a week in Canada at a whitewater school. After learning and practicing advanced paddling techniques, we decided to take an impromptu trip down Ontario's Kopka River on our way home to Montana.

> Credit: Terry Manier

I was lying in the flush pond when our canoe drifted next to me. I mustered enough strength to bail it out and pushed myself to the river's edge to rest. For about 45 minutes I waited and watched. My heart raced and my anxiety grew. It was all I could do to not lose it. But after having waited as long as I did, I knew something had gone terribly wrong. I couldn't wait any more.

A switch flipped. My scrambled mind snapped into utter rationality about my situation: I needed to move. It felt strange, at first, my complete lack of anxiety coupled with a disconnect from all emotion. But everything had become clear.

Tall canyon cliffs rose from the river on both sides. I tied the boat up to a tree so if Jane came out she'd know I was OK. My leg was slightly crooked and pounding, but my brain didn't register the pain. I grabbed a white bag from the canoe, hoping I could use it as a distress signal, fashioned a leg splint out of a balsam branch, and took a paddle to use as a crutch. I stumbled and crawled, dragging myself up the cliff on the east side of the rapids to look for Jane. In forty minutes I traveled no more than 100 yards. From the top of the cliff I scanned the rapids, searching for any sign of Jane. I crept to the cliff's edge and fell through a moss-covered hole before arresting myself on a balsam tree. I pulled myself back onto the rock, but I had seen nothing.

I dragged myself back down to the water's edge. The nearest highway was 2.5 miles away. I needed to get there. I followed the river. My body was in shock and hypothermia was creeping in. It was no more than 50°F, and a steady drizzle kept me soaked through.

I had to cross the river to get to the highway. I finally came upon a section that opened into a large lake of sorts, with an island in the middle. I was a mile from the road. My plan was to let the river carry me to the island, rest there, then get back in the river and cross to the other side. But 5 yards from the island, I got caught in a current that pulled me far out into the lake. Back-paddling my way toward the shore, the cold became unbearable. Then, across the lake, I spotted a boat.

I screamed, whistled, and slapped the water, but the motor was running, and the men didn't hear me. A few minutes later, they killed the engine to fish where the river flowed into the lake. I whistled again, grabbed the white plastic bag from my pocket, and tied it to my canoe-paddle crutch, waving it frantically in the air. They finally saw me. The men came over, hauled me into the boat, and brought me to their camp.

Fear Into Sadness

The paramedics came. I was hypothermic and my leg was snapped in three places. My logical, emotionless mind crumbled. The anxiety returned. Jane never did.

A few weeks later, search and rescue teams found Jane's body. The autopsy showed there was no water in her lungs. She had most likely hit her head on a rock when she went over. She had been gone instantly.

For months, I obsessed over details of the accident, wishing we hadn't decided to impulsively stop for the trip down the Kopka; wishing we had paddled just a bit harder to the right, avoiding the boulder we breached. As experienced wilderness travelers, we always knew there was some level of risk. And so many times we had walked out of the wilderness unscathed. So many times those trips had filled us with happiness.

A few days before the accident, Jane had turned to me and spontaneously said, "You know if something ever happens to me, you'll scatter my ashes in my five favorite wilderness places." We ran through them together. Then, all of a sudden, she was actually gone.

But that promise to her brought me through the grief and the guilt. I've fulfilled her last wish.

fire building/starting, *32*, 32–34; fire-starter materials for, 44–48, *45*, *47*, 57, 93, 176, 227, 253; fuel types for, 36–40, *37*, *41*, 56; "fuzz" sticks for, 144; hand drill and fire bow for, 54–56, *55*, 253; headlamp hacks for, 209; ice magnifying glass for, 176; igniters for, 52–54, *53*; kindling "bouquet" for, 56; preparation tips for, 38–40; rings for, *34*, 35–36; rules for, 52; for signaling, 38, 93, 142, 147; site locations and preparation for, 18, *34*, 35–36; structure types for, 48–51, *50*, *51*; tinder types and sources for, 36, *41*, *42*, 42–44, 46, 62, 93; trench, 15; for water boiling/cleaning, 83; in wet conditions, 40; wind protection for, 36; wood processing for, 145

fire maintenance, *63*; extinguishing tips for, 60–61, *61*, 62; fuel placement for, *58*, 58–59, *59*

fires, wild, 60, 196, 197–98

first aid, 148, *148*, 209; for altitude sickness, 167; for animal/insect injury, 169, 171–72; for ankle sprains/breaks, 165–66, *173*; for bone breaks, *154*, 154–58, *157*, *158*, 165–66, 253; for burns, 162, *163*; for dental injuries, 165; for external bleeding/wounds, 158–61, *173*; for frostbite, 168; hacks from everyday items, 172; for head injury, 150–51; for heart attacks, 164–65; for heat stroke/exhaustion, 89, 168; for hypothermia, 167; with ice, 176; for internal bleeding, 153–54; kit essentials, 170; for lung injuries, 162, 164, *164*; monitoring and note taking with, *173*, 173–75; natural remedies for, 175; RICE rule in, 166; for spine/neck injury, 152–53, *153*, 155; for sunburn, 168

fish and fishing, 101, *108*, 113, 231; books/paper for, 57; can or bottle hack for, 121; cleaning/gutting process for, *111*, 111–12; cooking whole over filleting, 112; headlamp hacks for, 209, *209*; roll casting for, 109–10; tackle box for, 107; tools and techniques for, 104, *105*, *106*, 106–10

fitness and physical ability, 232, *233*; assessment of, 233–35; balance exercises for, 245–46; body temperature control with, 235; core/back exercises for, 240, *240*; for feet, 244; for knees, 245; limberness stretches for, 246–52, *247–52*; lower/core exercises for, 236–38, *236–38*; 10-minute workout for, 242–43, *242–43*; upper/core exercises for, 238–40, *238–40*

floats, 206

floods, flash, 196, 201–2, *202*

food: bear bag/canisters for, 193, 195; carrion as, 120, *120*; dehydration avoidance and tips for, 71, 81; mental reaction with lack of, 95–96; preservation, 24; rules for edible wild, 102–3; scouting for wild, 96–97; spice kit for, 115; survival statistics without, 94; wild fruits for, 100, *100*, 124; wild greens for, 97, 98; wild protein sources, 101, *108*,

102–3; water sources from scouting, 74; water sourcing from, 81, 93; wild food sources from, *97*, 97–100, *99*, *100*, 124

pocketknives and multitools, *111*, 111–12

poisoning, 102–3, 116, 119, 168

Polaris. *See* North Star

poles, 201; for evacuation, 179; for river crossing, 207; slope assessment with, 197; for splints, 158, *158*

potholes (tinajas), *73*, 74

precipitation, 40; clouds signifying, *25*, 25–29, *27*; harvesting, 24

protein sources, 101, *108*, 116–19. *See also* fish and fishing; hunting

rain. *See* precipitation

rapids, 254–55

ravines. *See* canyons/ravines

reflective objects/materials, 24, 140–41, *141*, 143, 145, 227, 253

rescue: assessment and methods for, *151*, *152*, 177, *178*, 179; in bad weather, 183; patience with, 140, 147; rules for aiding, 142. *See also* evacuation; signaling

RICE first aid rule, 166

rivers: accidents, 254–55; crossings, 207

rock climbing, 30–31, *216*; rope hacks for survival, 204, *204*; threats, 185–86

rockfall, 200; avoiding, 198–99; death from, 185–86

rocks, hot, 84–85

roly-poly. *See* woodlice

rope: duct tape, 253, *253*; hacks for, 204, *204*

Rosenthal, Ed, 90–93, *92*

Salant, Pamela, 122–23

saw, 22–23

scorpions, 119

Scotty Bobs, 242, *242*

Shaul, Rob, 242

shelters, 12–13, *13*, 176; A-frame, 16–17, *17*; bed of leaves as, 14, *14*; bivy sack, 19–20, 65; location scouting for, 17–18; snow, *20*, 21–23, *22*; socks and anchoring, 87; space blankets for, 17, *17*, 24, *24*; tarp, 15, *15*; under trees, 14, 18, 182

shock, 161

shovel, 22–23

shuttle runs, 243, *243*

signaling, 31, *140*; books/paper for, 57; with fire, 38, 93, 142, 147; ice for, 176; with light, 143–45, 209; with reflection, 140–41, *141*, 143, 145, 227, 253; with sound, 139–40; space blanket for, 24

sleeping bag, 24

snakes, 87, 101, 171, *187*, 189

snares, 115

snow: blindness, *166*, 167; eating, 82; melting, 24; shelters, *20*, 21–23, *22*. *See also* avalanches

snowshoeing, 11–12

SOAP note (first-aid), 174

sock(s) hacks, 87

soda can fishing hack, 121

solar still, 80, *80*

SOS sign, 54, 141, 144–45

space blankets: as bivy sack, 20, 65; in shelter construction, 17, *17*, 24, *24*; survival hacks with, 24, *24*

spears, 104, *105*, 114–15, 145

spice kit, 115

spiders, *169*, 171, *187*, 189

spine/neck injury, 152–53, *153*, 155, 180–83

splints, *154*, 154–58, *157*, *158*, 209, 253

starches, 98–99, *99*

stars: navigation by, 136, *137*, 137–38; time determination by, 139

steel wool, 44, 53

step-ups, 243, *243*

SteriPENs, 86

sticks, 253; direction/navigation with, 136; "fuzz," 144; for shelter toggles, 15, *15*, 16, *16*; for spears, 104, *105*, 114–15, 145

stinkbugs, 119

storms. *See* weather

straw. *See* survival straw

stretcher, 179

stretches, 246–52, *247–52*

sunburn, 168

sun filter (water), 86

sunscreen, 88

surgeon's knot , *157*, 157

survival stories: boating accident, 254–55;

fall and paralysis, 180–83; grizzly attack, *210–11*, 210–13; lost and blind on Appalachian Trail, 146–47; lost in Alaskan blizzard, 64–67; lost in desert, 90–93, 125–27; lost with broken leg, 122–23; mantras in, 222; mental/emotional fear, 228–31; rock climbing, 30–31

survival straw, 74

tackle box, 107

tampons, utility of, 62, 159

tape, 155–56, 159, 160. *See also* duct tape

tarps, *15*, 15–16, *16*

teamwork, 11–12

termites, 118

thirst. *See* dehydration; water, drinking

threats, 184, *184*; elemental, *196*, 196–208, *199*, *202*, *203*, *205*; from insects, 169, *169*, 171–72, *187*, 189; mental/emotional reactions as, 214–16, 228–31; rock climbing, 185–86; rules for turning back when facing, 225; wildlife, 186, *187*, 188–95, 197. *See also* bears

ticks, 171, *187*, 189

time determination, 139

tinajas. *See* potholes

tinder. *See* fire building/starting

Tinder-Quik, 46

toggles, stick, 15, *15*, 16, *16*

topo map, *128*, 128–29, *129*

transpiration bag, 81, *81*

// ABOUT THE AUTHOR

Ted Alvarez is *BACKPACKER* magazine's Northwest Editor and was a National Magazine Award finalist in 2014. Whether chasing grizzly bears in the North Cascades, fording an icy Alaska river, or drinking his own urine in the desert, he regularly goes to extreme lengths in pursuit of a good story—often in our national parks. He lives in Seattle, Wash., where he survives on heroic doses of strong coffee.